EVERY FIGHT IS NOT YOUR FIGHT

NARESH CHANDRA NAYAK

NewDelhi • London

BLUEROSE PUBLISHERS
India | U.K.

Copyright © Naresh Chandra Nayak 2024

All rights reserved by author. No part of this publication may be reproduced, stored in a retrieval system, or transmitted in any form or by any means, electronic, mechanical, photocopying, recording or otherwise, without the prior permission of the author. Although every precaution has been taken to verify the accuracy of the information contained herein, the publisher assumes no responsibility for any errors or omissions. No liability is assumed for damages that may result from the use of information contained within.

BlueRose Publishers takes no responsibility for any damages, losses, or liabilities that may arise from the use or misuse of the information, products, or services provided in this publication.

For permissions requests or inquiries regarding this publication, please contact:

BLUEROSE PUBLISHERS
www.BlueRoseONE.com
info@bluerosepublishers.com
+91 8882 898 898
+4407342408967

ISBN: 978-93-6783-518-0

Cover design: Shubham
Typesetting: Sagar

First Edition: December 2024

Dedication

To Mrs. Angela Hallensleben,

From the heart of Germany, your unwavering kindness, support, and friendship have been a constant source of inspiration in my journey. Your compassion and wisdom have enriched my life, and this work is a small reflection of the profound impact you've made on my path. Thank you for believing in me.

Foreword

It is a great privilege to write the foreword for this profound and thought-provoking book. I have had the pleasure of knowing Fr. Naresh Chandra CM not only as a writer but as a person deeply committed to his faith and the well-being of others. As a German reader and an admirer of his previous work, "Weaving Lives: Essence of Human Connection," I have been inspired by his ability to bridge cultural and spiritual divides, weaving together narratives that resonate across boundaries and bring out the essence of our shared humanity.

In this book, Fr. Naresh explores a topic that is both timeless and deeply relevant: the nature of struggle and the discernment needed to choose our battles wisely. Drawing on his rich knowledge of biblical teachings and his own life experiences, he invites us to reflect on the deeper purpose of our struggles and the role of faith in navigating them.

As someone who has grappled with the complexities of faith and life's challenges in my own journey, I found this book to be a powerful guide. It reminds us that not every conflict demands our engagement, and that sometimes, the greatest wisdom lies in knowing when to step back and trust in a higher power. This message resonates deeply in our modern world, where we are often overwhelmed by the pressure to respond to every challenge, to be constantly active and in control.

Fr. Naresh's reflections offer a much-needed perspective of hope, faith, and discernment. He encourages us to align our actions with a greater purpose, to balance personal effort with divine reliance, and to find peace in the understanding that not every battle is ours to fight. His words serve as a gentle reminder that even in the face of overwhelming odds, goodness ultimately prevails when we act with righteousness and integrity.

In my own life, I have experienced the truth of these teachings. Through personal trials and the wisdom gained from faith, I have learned the value of letting go and trusting in something greater than myself. This book beautifully articulates the importance of this trust, drawing from the rich tapestry of religious wisdom and personal stories that Fr. Naresh so eloquently shares.

As the German poet Hermann Hesse once wrote, "Geduld ist alles!" which translates to, "Patience is everything!" This simple yet profound quote captures the essence of this book. It reminds us that in our struggles, patience, faith, and discernment are key. They allow us to see beyond immediate challenges and to trust in the unfolding of a greater plan. Just as patience transforms a rough stone into a polished gem, so too can our faith transform us through life's trials.

I believe this book will be a source of strength and guidance for many, offering a path of discernment and faith in the midst of life's complexities. It is a testament to the power of spiritual wisdom to illuminate our path, helping us to understand that, while we are called to act with courage and conviction, we are also invited to rest in the assurance that we are not alone in our struggles.

I hope that you, dear reader, will find in these pages the same inspiration and peace that I have found. May this book guide you in your own journey, helping you to navigate your struggles with wisdom, faith, and the assurance that the ultimate victory belongs to the forces of good.

Angela Hallensleben
Germany

Prologue

"Every Fight is Not Your Fight"

There comes a moment in every person's life when they stand at the crossroads of struggle and surrender, when the weight of the world presses upon their soul, and they must ask, "Is this battle mine to fight?" I have stood at that crossroad myself, feeling the tension between the urge to confront and the wisdom to let go. In those moments, the lessons of ancient teachings whisper to us, reminding us that not every fight is ours, and that sometimes, the greatest act of courage is in choosing which struggles to face and which to leave to the divine.

The world spins, and we often mistake the noise around us for a call to arms. Yet, as Shakespeare wrote in Hamlet, "Give thy thoughts no tongue, nor any unproportioned thought his act." Every stirring of the heart is not a command to fight. Just as not every storm is a disaster, not every struggle requires us to take up arms. This is a truth that has come to me through the trials of my own life. There have been battles I waged out of pride or impatience, and there have been moments where I stepped back and witnessed something far greater at work, unseen hands shaping outcomes far beyond my power.

In this book, we explore the timeless wisdom of the world's great religious and spiritual texts—words that have been lifelines for countless souls navigating their own battles. From the Bible to the Quran, the Bhagavad Gita to the Ramayana, the Mahabharata to the teachings of Buddha, we learn that life's greatest battles are often not fought with swords or might, but with inner strength, patience, and faith. It is not the size of the fight that matters, but the purpose behind it.

In my own journey, I have found solace in the words of the Bible: "The battle is not yours, but God's" (2 Chronicles 20:15). How often have we taken up burdens that were never ours to carry? How many sleepless nights have we spent, wrestling with forces we cannot control? We become, as John Milton so beautifully wrote in Paradise Lost, "With ruin upon ruin, rout on rout, Confusion worse confounded." But when we align our struggles with a higher purpose—when we fight for justice, for the good of others, and not just for our own pride—then the invincible, divine power fights for us.

The Quran teaches patience in the face of adversity, urging us to endure with grace and trust in God's plan. I have experienced this personally, during moments when life seemed unbearable, when I questioned my strength to go on. Yet, time and again, it was in my surrender, in trusting that something greater was at work, that the way became clear. It reminds me of the poignant line from T.S. Eliot: "I said to my soul, be still, and wait without hope, for hope would be hope for the wrong thing." In surrender, we find strength; in stillness, we find our true fight.

The Bhagavad Gita tells us that we must act, but without attachment to the outcome. In Arjuna's dilemma, as he stands at the battlefield of Kurukshetra, unsure whether to fight, I have found myself mirrored. His struggle is our struggle, and Krishna's wisdom to him is our wisdom: We must fight for righteousness, but the outcome is not in our hands. It is the journey, the righteous action, that defines us—not victory or defeat.

Each of these sacred texts echoes a common truth: when we align our struggles with a higher purpose, when we fight for justice, for the good of others, and not merely for our own gain, we are never truly alone. As I reflect on my own life, I can see the quiet moments of divine intervention, where, unbeknownst to me, the battle was being fought on my behalf. As the poet Rumi said, "Do not be satisfied with stories, how things have gone with others. Unfold your own myth." When we step into our own path, guided by wisdom and righteousness, we invite the divine to walk alongside us.

This book is a journey through the wisdom of the ages, reflecting on the battles fought by saints, prophets, warriors, and ordinary people. It is about understanding that not every challenge is meant to be faced head-on, but with wisdom, patience, and trust in a higher power. For in the end, it is not the strength of the fighter that determines victory, but the righteousness of the cause.

So, as we embark on this journey together, let us remember the words of W.B. Yeats: "In dreams begins responsibility." The dreams we chase, the battles we choose, are ours alone to bear—but not every battle is ours to win. Sometimes, we must trust in something greater. When we fight for the good, for truth and justice, we may find that the most powerful ally in our struggle is not ourselves, but the divine force that guides us all.

Contents

Dedication iii
Foreword iv
Prologue vii

Introductions 1
1. The Bible-Trusting in God's Justice 7
2. Enduring with Patience and Faith 14
3. The Struggle for Righteousness 22
4. The Quran – The Strength of Patience and Perseverance 32
5. Lord Rama's Fight for Justice and Righteousness 40
6. The Struggle for Justice and Righteous Leadership 49
7. Enduring Suffering with Hope and Conviction 59
8. The Mahabharata –
The Complexity of Battle and Moral Dilemmas 68
9. The Taoism – The Power of
Non-Resistance and Harmony 77
10. Buddhist Teachings –
The Middle Path and Non-Attachment 85
11. Myths and Legends –
Symbolic Battles and Their Moral Lessons 93
12. When God Fights for Us –
The Role of Divine Assistance 101
13. Lessons on Discernment –
Not Every Fight Is Your Fight 110
14. Conclusion: Understanding Your
Role in the Struggle for Good 118
About the Book 125
Reader Reviews 126
About the Author 128

Introductions

"In every battle, there comes a time when both sides consider themselves beaten, then he who continues the fight wins."
— Ulysses S. Grant

The Wisdom of Choosing Your Battles

Life is full of challenges—some we willingly accept, and others are thrust upon us. Whether in our personal lives, careers, relationships, or communities, we often feel compelled to fight for what we believe is right. But amid this struggle, a profound truth emerges: not every fight is yours to fight.

This realisation is one that transcends time, culture, and faith. Across the world's great religious and spiritual traditions, the idea of discernment—choosing which battles to engage in and which to leave in the hands of a higher power—is a recurring theme. When we step back, seeking wisdom rather than rushing into conflict, we often find that some struggles are not meant to be fought with sheer willpower alone. Instead, they require patience, trust, and an understanding that the universe, or God, fights for us when we align ourselves with righteousness and goodness.

I, like many of you, have experienced the emotional turbulence of taking on battles that were not mine to fight. At times, I fought simply because the situation demanded immediate action, or because my ego refused to let go. Yet, there were also moments when stepping back allowed the situation to resolve itself in ways I could not have imagined. In those moments, I realised the power of surrender, not as a sign of defeat, but as a deeper recognition that we are not always the authors of the outcomes we seek.

This book, "Not Every Fight is Your Fight," draws upon the ancient wisdom found in the Bible, the Quran, the Bhagavad Gita, the Ramayana, the Mahabharata, and other sacred teachings. These texts have been guiding lights for countless individuals throughout history, offering clarity in times of conflict and uncertainty. The teachings they impart are as relevant today as they were centuries ago, helping us navigate the complexity of modern life and the struggles we face.

The Fight Within: Understanding Inner and Outer Battles

Every human being faces two kinds of battles: the outer struggles, which involve the world around us, and the inner battles, which take place within our minds and hearts. The Bible, for example, speaks to this inner conflict when it says, *"For we do not wrestle against flesh and blood, but against the rulers, against the authorities, against the powers of this dark world" (Ephesians 6:12).* Often, the fight is not against external enemies but against our own fears, doubts, and insecurities.

Similarly, in the Bhagavad Gita, Arjuna's battle is not only against the enemies standing before him on the battlefield, but also against the turmoil within his soul. He questions whether fighting his own kin is truly just, whether the cause is worth the cost. Krishna's guidance to Arjuna, urging him to act according to his **Dharma** (duty) without attachment to the outcome, speaks to the heart of this universal struggle.

The same themes appear in the Quran, where endurance, patience, and faith are seen as crucial in facing both external challenges and internal doubts. The Prophet Yusuf (Joseph) endured betrayal, imprisonment, and injustice, yet he never allowed the circumstances of his life to dictate the condition of his soul. Through his story, we learn that sometimes the most significant battles are those where we simply remain steadfast, trusting that God is in control.

The Fight for Justice: When Is It Righteous?

At the heart of many religious teachings is the notion of fighting for justice, not just for oneself but for others. This is not about selfish ambition or personal gain, but about standing up for righteousness, even when the odds are against you. In the Ramayana, Lord Rama's battle against the demon king Ravana was not a personal vendetta, but a fight to restore *order, justice, and honour.*

His struggle was for the greater good, not for personal glory.

Similarly, in the Bible, David did not fight Goliath because of personal pride, but because Goliath represented a threat to the people of Israel. David's faith in God gave him the strength to face an opponent much stronger than him. This story teaches us that when we fight for a righteous cause, we are never truly fighting alone. As in 1 Samuel 17:47 it is written, *"The battle is the Lord's"*.

In the Quran, the concept of Jihad is often misunderstood. While it can mean a physical struggle for justice, its primary meaning is the internal, personal struggle for righteousness and self-purification. The Prophet Muhammad himself emphasised the importance of this "**greater Jihad**," the battle to overcome one's own flaws and strive for goodness. This teaches us that the most important battles are not always external, but the daily fight to remain honest, kind, and faithful in the face of adversity.

When Not to Fight: The Wisdom of Letting Go

In contrast, there are times when we are called not to fight at all. The **Tao Te Ching**, a foundational text of Taoism, speaks about the power of **non-action, or Wu Wei**. It teaches that sometimes the best way to handle a situation is by not resisting, by letting the natural flow of the universe take its course. **"The soft overcomes the hard,"** it says, pointing out that yielding, rather than pushing, can often lead to greater success.

Buddhism also teaches the importance of **non-attachment**, a concept that extends to our struggles. The Buddha, in his wisdom, showed that many of our battles stem from desires and attachments that cause suffering. By learning to let go, by not clinging to every conflict or perceived injustice, we find peace. This does not mean turning away from the world's problems, but rather approaching them with a calm and steady heart, knowing that we cannot control everything.

The Divine Fight: When God Fights for You

One of the most comforting truths across all religious traditions is the belief that when you fight for what is good and just, you are not alone. God, or the divine power, fights alongside you, sometimes even in ways you cannot see. In the Bible, we see countless examples of this—whether it's Moses leading the Israelites out of Egypt with divine assistance, or the angels descending to aid the believers in the Battle of Badr, as described in the Quran. When the fight is righteous, there is a sense of divine protection and guidance.

This idea resonates in Hinduism as well. In the **Mahabharata, the Pandavas** are guided by **Lord Krishna,** who represents divine will and wisdom. Though they are outnumbered, their cause is just, and ultimately, it is this moral righteousness, combined with Krishna's divine intervention, that leads them to victory.

We also see this in other spiritual traditions, from the teachings of indigenous cultures, which emphasise living in harmony with the divine forces of nature, to the moral lessons of mythologies worldwide. The notion is clear: when you are aligned with righteousness, the universe conspires to support you.

Learning to Discern: Not Every Fight is Yours

The challenge, then, is to learn which battles are truly ours. In a world filled with noise, conflict, and endless opportunities for confrontation, it takes wisdom to discern which struggles are worthy of our energy and which are better left in the hands of God.

This book aims to guide you through that discernment, offering the wisdom of the world's most sacred texts as a roadmap. Together, we will explore how to choose your battles with care, how to fight with courage and conviction when the cause is just, and how to surrender with grace when the fight is not yours. We will learn that strength lies not only in action but in the quiet wisdom of letting go, trusting that when we fight for what is right, the divine power will always fight for us.

As we embark on this journey, let us remember that the greatest battles are often those fought in the heart, and the greatest victories are not always won by force. Rather, they are won by faith, wisdom, and the understanding that not every fight is yours to fight. But when it is, you will not be fighting alone.

1

The Bible-Trusting in God's Justice

The Call to Discernment: Choosing Your Battles

> *"Do not be overcome by evil,*
> *but overcome evil with good."*
> — *(Romans 12:21)*

From the beginning, the Bible teaches us that life is filled with challenges and conflicts, but we are not always meant to fight every battle. There is a clear distinction between fights born out of ego and selfish desires, and those that arise from the call to justice and righteousness. Romans 12:19 offers a profound reminder: *"Beloved, never avenge yourselves, but leave room for the wrath of God; for it is written, 'Vengeance is mine, I will repay, says the Lord.'"*

This verse encapsulates the idea that some battles are best left to God. When we feel wronged or attacked, our natural instinct may be to fight back, to seek revenge, or to prove ourselves. But Scripture asks us to pause, to trust in God's ultimate justice, and to discern whether this battle is truly ours to fight. Often, by letting go of the need to control or retaliate, we leave room for God to intervene in ways that we cannot foresee.

I remember an experience from my early days as a priest when a rumour about me spread within the community. It was painful, and my first impulse was to defend myself and confront those who spoke against me. I spent days drafting responses in my head, imagining how I would clear my name. But during prayer, I felt a deep sense of peace and the words from Romans 12:19 came to mind. I decided to let go, trusting God to reveal the truth in His time. Weeks later, the person who had started the rumour came forward and apologised publicly. It was a humbling experience that taught me to trust in God's justice rather than my own need to vindicate myself.

David and Goliath: Fighting for a Cause Greater than Self

"You come to me with sword and spear and javelin; but I come to you in the name of the Lord of hosts, the God of the armies of Israel, whom you have defied."
— (1 Samuel 17:45)

One of the most iconic battles in the Bible is David's fight against Goliath. David, a young shepherd boy, faced a seasoned warrior who towered over him in size and strength. But David didn't fight for personal glory or out of ego. His battle was rooted in defending his people and upholding God's honour. 1 Samuel 17:45

recounts David's words to Goliath: "You come to me with sword and spear and javelin; but I come to you in the name of the Lord of hosts, the God of the armies of Israel, whom you have defied."

David's fight was not his own—it was for the good of his people and in defence of God's name. His victory was not because of his strength or skill, but because he placed his trust in God. David teaches us that when we fight for a cause greater than ourselves, we are never truly fighting alone. The fight becomes a righteous one, and God's power is with us.

This lesson resonates deeply with my own journey as a missionary. In my early years, I was assigned to a remote village in Odisha, where I faced significant resistance in trying to establish a school for underprivileged children. The challenges seemed insurmountable, and there were moments when I felt completely overwhelmed. But remembering David's courage, I realised that my mission was not for my own recognition but to serve a greater purpose. I prayed for strength and continued my work, despite the opposition. Eventually, the community came together, and we were able to build the school, providing education and hope to many. It was a victory that belonged to God, not to me.

Jesus' Teachings on Non-Retaliation and Loving Your Enemy

> *"But I say to you, love your enemies*
> *and pray for those who persecute you."*
> *(Matthew 5:44)*

Jesus' teachings in the New Testament further expand on this idea of discerning when to fight and when to let go. In the Sermon on the Mount, Jesus says, *"You have heard that it was said, 'An eye for an eye and a tooth for a tooth.' But I say to you, Do not resist an evildoer. But if anyone strikes you on the right cheek, turn the other also"* - (Matthew 5:38-39). This radical teaching challenges our natural instincts for revenge and retaliation. Jesus is not encouraging passivity in the face of injustice, but rather inviting us to think deeply about the nature of the conflicts we engage in.

In a world where conflict seems unavoidable *whether in personal relationships or on a global scale* Jesus asks us to consider the power of non-retaliation. Turning the other cheek is not about being weak; it is about choosing a different kind of strength. It's about recognising that not every offence demands a fight. By choosing love over retaliation, we leave room for transformation both in ourselves and in others.

I recall a difficult encounter with a fellow companion. We had a significant disagreement over a community issue, and the tension between us grew. Every part of me wanted to argue my point and defend my position. But in my prayer, I felt called to let go and listen. I chose to approach him, not with accusations, but with a genuine desire to understand his perspective. This small act of humility transformed our relationship. We were able to find common ground, and our work together flourished. It reminded me that sometimes, choosing not to fight is the most powerful response.

Trusting in God's Timing and Justice

> *"For everything there is a season, and a time for every matter under heaven."*
> *—(Ecclesiastes 3:1)*

Throughout the Bible, we see examples of individuals who trusted in God's timing rather than taking matters into their own hands. Abraham waited decades for the fulfilment of God's promise for a son. Joseph endured years of imprisonment and injustice before rising to power in Egypt. In each of these stories, we are reminded that God's justice and timing are perfect, even when they don't align with our own expectations.

In today's world, where we often feel the pressure to act quickly and decisively, it can be difficult to wait on God. Whether it's waiting for justice in a broken system, or simply waiting for resolution in a personal conflict, the temptation to take matters into our own hands is strong. But Scripture continually encourages us to trust that God sees what we cannot and that His justice is always working, even when it seems delayed.

There was a time when I was deeply frustrated by the lack of progress in a project I was leading. Despite my best efforts, everything seemed to be at a standstill. I prayed fervently for a breakthrough, but nothing changed. One day, as I was reflecting on Ecclesiastes 3:1, I felt a sense of peace wash over me. I realised that God's timing was not my timing, and that I needed to trust that things would unfold as they were meant to. A few months later, new resources and opportunities came our way, and the project moved forward more smoothly than I could have imagined. It was a powerful reminder that God's timing is indeed perfect.

Present-Day Realities: When to Fight and When to Trust

> *"Speak out for those who cannot speak,*
> *for the rights of all the destitute."*
> *— (Proverbs 31:8)*

In our current world, conflicts abound political divisions, social justice issues, and personal disagreements are all around us. Knowing when to engage and when to step back is more important than ever. The Bible provides a blueprint for navigating these conflicts with wisdom. It teaches us that not every fight is ours to fight and that sometimes, the most righteous act is to trust in God's justice rather than seeking our own.

One present-day example is the rise of social justice movements around the world. Activists and advocates fight for equality, fairness, and the protection of the vulnerable. Their battles are aligned with the biblical call to "Speak out for those who cannot speak, for the rights of all the destitute" (Proverbs 31:8). Yet, even in these righteous causes, there is a need for discernment to know when to act and when to trust that God is working behind the scenes.

It's worth taking the case of Nelson Mandela, who fought against apartheid in South Africa. His battle was long and difficult, marked by imprisonment and personal sacrifice. Yet, Mandela often spoke of his reliance on God's justice and timing. Even when he was in prison, unable to physically fight against the oppression, he trusted that his cause was just and that in time, God's justice would prevail. And it did.

Conclusion: The Power of Trusting God's Justice

"Wait for the Lord; be strong, and let your heart take courage; wait for the Lord!"
— (Psalm 27:14)

The Bible teaches us that life will inevitably present us with battles, but not all of them are ours to fight. The stories of David, Joseph, and Jesus remind us that sometimes, the greatest strength lies in discernment and trust. When we align ourselves with God's will and fight for righteousness, we do not fight alone. And when the battle is not ours to fight, we can rest in the assurance that God's justice will prevail in His time.

In today's world, filled with noise and conflict, this lesson is more relevant than ever. By learning to choose our battles wisely, trusting in God's justice, and letting go of the need for personal vindication, we not only find peace for ourselves but also become part of God's greater plan for justice and goodness in the world.

2

Enduring with Patience and Faith

The Virtue of Patience: Trusting in God's Timing

"Be still before the Lord, and wait patiently for Him; do not fret over those who prosper in their way, over those who carry out evil devices."
— *(Psalm 37:7)*

Patience is one of the most emphasised virtues in the Bible. Throughout scripture, believers are encouraged to trust in God's timing, even when life feels overwhelming and unjust. Patience, in the biblical sense, is not just about waiting; it's about having faith that God is in control and that His plans will unfold at the right time. James 1:3-4 says, "Because you know that the testing of your faith produces perseverance. Let perseverance finish its work so that you may be mature and complete, not lacking anything."

This passage reminds us that life's trials are opportunities for growth. The challenges we face are not random, nor are they meant to break us. Instead, they serve as tests of faith, opportunities to build character, and deepen our relationship with God. When we respond with patience, we show our trust in God's larger plan, even when we cannot see the outcome.

I recall a difficult time early in my ministry when I felt a strong calling to serve in a specific community, but obstacles kept appearing. Every door I tried to open seemed to close in my face. I prayed fervently for guidance and clarity, but the answers didn't come as quickly as I had hoped. During this period, I held onto Psalm 37:7, "Be still before the Lord, and wait patiently for Him." This verse became my anchor. Eventually, an unexpected opportunity arose that allowed me to serve in that community in a way I had never imagined, fulfilling my calling more deeply than I thought possible. This experience taught me that God's timing is always perfect, even when it feels delayed.

The Story of Job: A Testament to Unshakeable Faith

"You have heard of the endurance of Job, and you have seen the purpose of the Lord, how the Lord is compassionate and merciful."
— (James 5:11)

If there is one figure in the Bible who embodies patience and endurance, it is Job. His story is one of unimaginable suffering, loss, and pain. Job was a righteous man, yet he lost his wealth, his children, and his health in a series of devastating events. His friends and even his wife urged him to curse God and abandon his faith. But Job's response was a profound testament to patience and trust. In Job 1:21, he declares, "The Lord gave, and the Lord has taken away; blessed be the name of the Lord."

Job's unwavering faith in the face of suffering teaches us that patience is not just about waiting for the storm to pass but about trusting God even in the midst of the storm. His story reminds us that God's plan is often beyond our understanding, and that suffering, while painful, can serve a greater purpose. James 5:11 reflects on Job's endurance, saying, "Indeed we call blessed those who showed endurance. You have heard of the endurance of Job, and you have seen the purpose of the Lord, how the Lord is compassionate and merciful."

In today's world, where many face their own "Job-like" trials—prolonged illness, the loss of loved ones, or financial hardship—Job's example encourages believers to remain steadfast in faith, even when answers aren't immediately clear. I once met a family who had lost everything in a natural disaster. Their home, their possessions, everything they had worked for was gone. Yet, in the face of this devastation, they held onto their faith, believing that God would restore them in His time. Their resilience and trust reminded me of Job, and how enduring faith can see us through even the darkest times.

Jesus' Example of Patience and Forgiveness

"When He was abused, He did not return abuse; when He suffered, He did not threaten; but He entrusted Himself to the one who judges justly."
— *(1 Peter 2:23)*

The ultimate example of patience in the Bible is found in Jesus Christ. Throughout His life and ministry, Jesus faced rejection, betrayal, and suffering, yet He remained patient and obedient to God's will. One of the most striking examples of this is His response during His crucifixion. As He was unjustly nailed to the cross, He did not retaliate or curse those who persecuted Him. Instead, He prayed, "Father, forgive them, for they do not know what they are doing" (Luke 23:34).

Jesus' endurance and patience in the face of unimaginable pain and injustice is a model for how we should respond to our own struggles. He teaches us that even in moments of profound suffering, we are called to forgive and to trust in God's plan. This is particularly relevant in today's world, where social conflicts and personal betrayals can leave us feeling wronged. Jesus' example challenges us to rise above our natural instincts for revenge and instead, respond with love, patience, and faith.

I once had a close friend who betrayed my trust in a significant way. I was hurt, angry, and felt justified in cutting off the relationship entirely. But as I reflected on Jesus' words from the cross, I realised that I was being called to a higher standard. Instead of responding with bitterness, I chose to forgive and open the door to reconciliation. It wasn't easy, and it took time, but that act of patience and forgiveness not only healed our friendship but also transformed me. It reminded me that true strength is found in patience, humility, and love.

Present-Day Realities: Patience in the Face of Injustice

> *"Rejoice in hope, be patient in suffering, persevere in prayer."— (Romans 12:12)*

In our fast-paced world, where instant gratification is often expected, the Bible's emphasis on patience can feel counterintuitive. We want immediate answers to our prayers, quick solutions to our problems, and swift justice when we've been wronged. But the Bible repeatedly reminds us that God's timing is not our timing. Ecclesiastes 3:11 tells us, "He has made everything suitable for its time."

Consider the ongoing struggles for social justice across the globe. Movements like the fight for racial equality, gender rights, or the fight against poverty are not won overnight. Activists and leaders often work for years, or even decades, without seeing immediate results. Yet, they persist, trusting that justice will come in time. This patience, this long-suffering endurance, reflects the biblical call to persevere in doing good, even when the results are slow to materialise.

A present-day example of this is the story of Malala Yousafzai, who, after being shot by the Taliban for advocating for girls' education, continued her fight with patience and resilience. Despite the threats and violence she faced, Malala persisted, becoming a global advocate for education and the youngest-ever Nobel Prize laureate. Her story is a powerful testament to the endurance of those who fight for justice, reflecting the spirit of Romans 12:12— "Rejoice in hope, be patient in suffering, persevere in prayer."

The Parable of the Persistent Widow: A Lesson in Faithful Persistence

"Will not God grant justice to His chosen ones who cry to Him day and night? Will He delay long in helping them?"
— (Luke 18:7)

In Luke 18:1-8, Jesus tells the parable of the persistent widow who continuously pleads with an unjust judge for justice. Though the judge initially refuses, her persistence eventually wears him down, and he grants her request. Jesus tells this story to teach us about the power of faithful persistence in prayer, saying, "And will not God grant justice to His chosen ones who cry to Him day and night? Will He delay long in helping them?" (Luke 18:7).

This parable highlights the importance of persistence—not just in action, but in prayer. It reminds us that while God's timing may seem slow by our standards, He hears our cries and will respond in His time. The widow's persistence mirrors our own struggles when we face repeated challenges, yet her eventual triumph assures us that God's justice will come, even if it requires patient endurance.

I remember a parishioner who prayed for years for the reconciliation of her family. Despite many setbacks and broken relationships, she never gave up hope. She prayed every day, trusting that God would heal the wounds and bring peace. After nearly a decade, her family came together in a way that only God could orchestrate. Her story reminded me of the persistent widow and the power of never losing hope, even when the wait seems long.

Conclusion: Patience as a Path to God's Justice

"Those who wait for the Lord shall renew their strength, they shall mount up with wings like eagles, they shall run and not be weary, they shall walk and not faint."
— (Isaiah 40:31)

The Bible teaches us that patience is not a passive act, but an active, faith-filled response to life's trials. Whether it's Job enduring unimaginable suffering, Jesus forgiving His persecutors, or the persistent widow seeking justice, we learn that patience is a powerful tool in our spiritual arsenal. Through patience, we align ourselves with God's timing and trust in His perfect plan.

In today's fast-paced world, where solutions are expected immediately, the Bible's emphasis on patience is a countercultural but necessary reminder that some battles take time. By cultivating patience and trusting in

God's justice, we can endure life's trials with faith, knowing that, as Isaiah 40:31 promises, "Those who wait for the Lord shall renew their strength; they shall mount up with wings like eagles; they shall run and not be weary; they shall walk and not faint."

The story of Job, the teachings of Jesus, and the parable of the persistent widow all point to this central truth: Not every fight is yours to fight in haste. Sometimes, the most righteous course of action is to wait, trust, and let God work in His time. Through patience, we find strength, wisdom, and ultimately, victory in God's greater plan.

3

The Struggle for Righteousness

The Battle Between Flesh and Spirit: Understanding Inner Conflict

"For the flesh desires what is contrary to the Spirit, and the Spirit what is contrary to the flesh. They are in conflict with each other, so that you are not to do whatever you want."
— (Galatians 5:17)

Throughout the Bible, believers are called to engage in a battle that is not just physical, but deeply spiritual—a battle between the flesh and the spirit, between human weakness and God's call to righteousness. This internal struggle is reflected in the words of Galatians 5:17: "For the flesh desires what is contrary to the Spirit, and the Spirit what is contrary to the flesh. They are in conflict with each other, so that you are not to do whatever you want."

This verse speaks to the core of the Christian life—an ongoing struggle between following our sinful, human inclinations and living according to God's will. We are often pulled in different directions, tempted by pride, anger, greed, or fear. Yet, the Bible reminds us that the true fight is not against external enemies, but against these internal forces that keep us from living a life of righteousness.

In my own experience, this internal conflict became particularly clear during a time when I struggled with pride. After receiving praise for a project I led, I found myself craving recognition and admiration, instead of directing glory to God. The more I sought personal validation, the more I felt disconnected from my spiritual calling. As I prayed and reflected on Scripture, I realised that the real battle was not with others, but within myself—between my ego and my desire to serve God selflessly. Romans 12:21, "Do not be overcome by evil, but overcome evil with good," reminded me that overcoming the temptation of pride required humility and surrender to God's will. It was a humbling lesson that taught me to prioritise righteousness over recognition.

This inner struggle is one that Christians face daily in various forms. Whether it's resisting the urge to gossip, battling jealousy, or overcoming addiction, the Bible teaches that these are the real battles we are called to fight. And though the struggle is constant, the power of the Holy Spirit strengthens us to overcome the flesh and walk in righteousness.

The Armour of God: Fighting the Battle for Righteousness

"Therefore, take up the whole armour of God, so that you may be able to withstand on that evil day, and having done everything, to stand firm."
— (Ephesians 6:13)

In Ephesians 6:10-18, the Apostle Paul writes about the importance of equipping ourselves with the "Armour of God" to fight against spiritual forces of evil. Paul reminds believers that our struggle is not against flesh and blood, but against the spiritual forces of darkness. He encourages us to put on the full armour of God to stand firm in this battle.

"Put on the whole armour of God, so that you may be able to stand against the wiles of the devil... Stand therefore, and fasten the belt of truth around your waist, and put on the breastplate of righteousness, and as shoes for your feet put on whatever will make you ready to proclaim the gospel of peace." (Ephesians 6:11, 14-15)

This passage presents a powerful metaphor for how we should prepare ourselves to fight for righteousness. The "belt of truth" represents our commitment to God's Word, grounding us in honesty and integrity. The "breastplate of righteousness" protects our hearts, keeping us pure and steadfast in our faith. The "gospel of peace" equips us to face conflict with calm assurance, rather than aggression. And finally, the "shield of faith" allows us to defend ourselves against the doubts and temptations that threaten our spiritual walk.

In a modern context, this armour equips believers to stand firm in a world where moral and spiritual challenges abound. Whether we face ethical dilemmas at work, struggle with personal integrity, or deal with cultural pressures that contradict our faith, the Armour of God helps us fight these battles with strength and wisdom.

I remember a time when I was tempted to compromise my integrity for the sake of approval. I was part of a team that was pressured to falsify reports to secure funding for a project. The easy path would have been to remain silent, to go along with what everyone else was doing. But as I prayed for guidance, the imagery of the Armour of God came to mind. The "belt of truth" reminded me that standing for honesty and integrity was my Christian duty, and the "breastplate of righteousness" gave me the courage to speak out. Confronting the issue was difficult, but through faith, I was able to stand firm in my commitment to what was right.

Jesus' Teachings on Righteousness: The Sermon on the Mount

> *"Blessed are those who hunger and thirst for righteousness, for they will be filled."*
> *— (Matthew 5:6)*

In the New Testament, Jesus teaches extensively about righteousness, particularly in His Sermon on the Mount. One of the most striking statements He makes is found in Matthew 5:6: "Blessed are those who hunger and thirst for righteousness, for they will be filled."

This teaching emphasises that the pursuit of righteousness is not a passive endeavour—it requires an active desire to seek justice, truth, and holiness. Jesus calls us to "hunger" and "thirst" for righteousness, suggesting that this pursuit should be a central focus of our lives. It is not enough to avoid doing wrong; we are called to actively seek what is good, to fight for justice, and to live in accordance with God's will.

The Sermon on the Mount also expands on what it means to live righteously in a world that is often hostile to those values. Matthew 5:10 says, "Blessed are those who are persecuted for righteousness' sake, for theirs is the kingdom of heaven." Jesus acknowledges that standing up for what is right may bring opposition, but He assures us that this struggle is not in vain. The reward for enduring these battles, both internal and external, is eternal and far greater than any temporary suffering we may face.

In today's world, this teaching remains deeply relevant. We live in a time when standing up for biblical values can lead to persecution, whether in the form of ridicule, social exclusion, or even legal challenges. But Jesus' promise of blessing for those who are persecuted because of righteousness encourages believers to remain steadfast, knowing that God sees and rewards their faithfulness.

I have witnessed this personally in my church community, where individuals have been mocked or criticised for their commitment to biblical principles. Yet, their faithfulness has been a powerful witness to others. One member, a public-school teacher, faced significant backlash for refusing to promote ideologies that conflicted with her Christian beliefs. Despite the pressure, she stood firm, living out Jesus' call to hunger and thirst for righteousness. Her perseverance inspired many, and while her stand for truth was met with challenges, it also opened doors for meaningful conversations about faith and integrity.

The Parable of the Persistent Widow: Perseverance in Seeking Justice

"And will not God grant justice to His chosen ones
who cry to Him day and night?
Will He delay long in helping them?"
— (Luke 18:7)

One of the clearest teachings on fighting for righteousness comes from Jesus' Parable of the Persistent Widow in Luke 18:1-8. In this story, Jesus tells of a widow who continually seeks justice from an unjust judge. Though the judge initially refuses her requests, her persistence eventually wears him down, and he grants her the justice she seeks. Jesus concludes the parable by saying, "And will not God bring about justice for His chosen ones, who cry out to Him day and night? Will He keep putting them off?"

This parable illustrates the importance of perseverance in the pursuit of justice. The widow's persistence is a model for how believers are called to engage in righteous struggles, particularly in the face of opposition. It reminds us that God is a just judge who will ultimately grant justice to those who seek it faithfully. However, the timing of this justice may not be immediate, and we are called to persevere in prayer and action until God's will is done.

In today's context, this perseverance is critical for those fighting systemic injustice—whether it's racial inequality, poverty, or other social issues. The persistence of activists and advocates who work tirelessly for justice mirrors the widow's determination in Jesus' parable. The fight for justice may be long and challenging, but the Bible assures us that God's justice will prevail in the end.

Consider the work of civil rights leaders like Dr. Martin Luther King Jr., who fought against racial injustice with both faith and persistence. His commitment to nonviolent protest and his deep belief in God's ultimate justice reflect the teachings of the Persistent Widow parable. Though the fight for civil rights was long and difficult, King's unwavering pursuit of righteousness inspired a movement that changed the course of history.

Present-Day Realities: Righteousness in a World of Injustice

> *"Let justice roll down like waters, and righteousness like an ever-flowing stream."*
> — *(Amos 5:24)*

The Bible's teachings on righteousness are not confined to ancient times; they are deeply relevant to the world we live in today. In a time when moral and ethical standards are often compromised for convenience or personal gain, the call to fight for righteousness remains as important as ever. Whether we are faced with personal dilemmas, professional challenges, or societal issues, the Bible urges us to pursue what is right, even when it is difficult.

We see examples of this in the ongoing struggles for justice around the world. Whether it's advocates fighting for human rights, environmental protection, or ethical leadership, the battle for righteousness is ongoing. The Bible's teachings on patience, persistence, and reliance on God's strength provide guidance and encouragement for those engaged in these modern-day battles.

One such example is the global fight against human trafficking. Organisations and individuals who combat this horrific crime often face overwhelming challenges and dangers. Yet, they continue to fight, fuelled by the belief that every life is precious and that God's justice will prevail. Their work is a powerful testament to the enduring struggle for righteousness and the unwavering belief in the sanctity of human life.

Conclusion: The Struggle for Righteousness is a Fight Worth Fighting

"Blessed are those who are persecuted for righteousness' sake, for theirs is the kingdom of heaven."
— *(Matthew 5:10)*

The Bible teaches us that the struggle for righteousness is both an internal and external battle. Whether we are fighting against our own sinful nature, standing up for truth and justice, or persevering in the face of opposition, the Bible provides a roadmap for how to engage in these struggles with faith, wisdom, and patience. From the Armour of God in Ephesians to the teachings of Jesus in the Sermon on the Mount, scripture equips us for the fight, assuring us that we do not fight alone.

As we navigate the complexities of the modern world, the Bible's call to hunger and thirst for righteousness remains as relevant as ever. It encourages us to fight not for our own gain, but for the greater good—for God's justice, truth, and peace. And in this fight, we are promised that even when the battle seems long, the obstacles overwhelming, or the opposition fierce, God is with us every step of the way.

Isaiah 40:31 reminds us, "But those who wait for the Lord shall renew their strength, they shall mount up with wings like eagles, they shall run and not be weary, they shall walk and not faint." This promise assures us that as we pursue righteousness, we are sustained by God's strength, not our own. Even when victory feels distant, the perseverance to continue is a testimony of faith, rooted in the belief that God's justice will ultimately prevail.

The struggle for righteousness is not always easy, but the Bible teaches us that it is a fight worth fighting. Whether we are standing up against personal injustices, speaking truth in a world filled with falsehoods, or living out our faith in difficult circumstances, we are called to endure with faith, knowing that the Lord's justice will one day triumph. As Jesus assures us in Matthew 5:10, "Blessed are those who are persecuted for righteousness' sake, for theirs is the kingdom of heaven."

Thus, in the face of every challenge, we can stand firm, knowing that God fights for us and with us, and that in the end, righteousness will be rewarded in His perfect timing.

4

The Quran – The Strength of Patience and Perseverance

The Role of Patience in Struggles

"Indeed, Allah is with the patient."
— *Quran 2:153*

In the Quran, one of the most emphasised virtues is patience, known as Sabr. Life, as depicted in the Quran, is filled with tests and trials, and the quality that enables believers to endure these challenges is patience. This form of patience is not passive resignation; rather, it is an active state of endurance, maintaining faith and trust in Allah's plan. The Quran 2:153 reminds believers of the importance of this virtue: "O you who have believed, seek help through patience and prayer. Indeed, Allah is with the patient."

This verse serves as a reminder that, in the face of adversity, the initial response should not be to retaliate or despair, but to seek strength through patience and prayer. Patience, in this context, is a form of inner resilience, a trust in God's timing and wisdom, allowing us to endure hardship without losing faith or hope.

I recall a personal experience during a time of intense financial instability that threatened my peace of mind. The urge to panic and react impulsively was strong, but I was reminded of the teachings of the Quran on Sabr. I realised that while I could not control every aspect of the situation, I could control my response. By practicing patience and turning to prayer, I found clarity and calm amidst the chaos, and eventually, the circumstances began to improve. The Quran teaches that by cultivating patience, we align ourselves with divine timing, trusting that the best outcomes will manifest in due time.

This concept of patience is vividly illustrated in the story of Prophet Yusuf (Joseph).

The Story of Prophet Yusuf: A Model of Patience and Perseverance

> *"Indeed, no one despairs of relief from Allah*
> *except the disbelieving people."*
> *— Quran 12:87*

Prophet Yusuf's life is one of the most profound examples of enduring trials with unwavering faith. Betrayed by his brothers, sold into slavery, and later imprisoned due to false accusations, Yusuf's life was marked by constant hardship. Yet, through it all, he maintained his trust in Allah. The Quran 12:87 captures his spirit of hope and resilience: "Indeed, no one despairs of relief from Allah except the disbelieving people."

Yusuf's story is not just a tale of suffering but a testament to the power of patience. Despite the injustices he faced, he never wavered in his faith or his integrity. Years later, when he was elevated to a position of power in Egypt, he demonstrated his strength of character by forgiving his brothers who had wronged him. His life teaches us that, even when we cannot see the larger picture, Allah is working behind the scenes, turning our trials into triumphs.

In today's world, Yusuf's story resonates with those who face unjust situations—whether it's wrongful imprisonment, social inequalities, or personal betrayals. The instinct to fight back and seek immediate justice is natural, but the Quran teaches us that patience and faith in Allah's wisdom can lead to outcomes far better than we could have imagined.

Consider the struggle of refugees displaced by conflict and war. Many have lost everything—homes, families, and livelihoods—yet they hold onto hope and faith in the face of overwhelming adversity. Their patience, much like Yusuf's, is a powerful testament to the endurance of the human spirit and the belief in Allah's ultimate justice. Although their struggle may seem never-ending, they find solace in the hope that Allah's mercy and justice will prevail in the end.

Jihad: The Inner and Outer Struggle

> *"And if you punish, punish with an equivalent punishment, but if you are patient—it is better for those who are patient."*
> — *(Quran 16:126)*

The concept of Jihad in the Quran is often misunderstood. While it is frequently associated with external conflict, its primary meaning refers to an inner, personal struggle—the effort to live a righteous life, to maintain faith, and to resist one's own negative impulses. This is known as the greater Jihad, or the struggle of the soul.

Quran 16:126 advises restraint even in situations of conflict: "And if you punish, punish with an equivalent punishment, but if you are patient—it is better for those who are patient." This verse highlights the importance of self-control, even when one is wronged. The greater Jihad requires immense discipline, as it calls on believers to combat their own anger, desire for revenge, and ego.

I experienced a personal moment of greater Jihad during a disagreement with a family member. The argument escalated quickly, and harsh words were exchanged. My initial reaction was to retaliate, but I remembered the Quran's emphasis on patience and self-restraint. Instead of escalating the conflict, I chose silence and calm. This approach not only defused the situation but also led to a peaceful resolution later. This small personal victory reminded me that the greatest battles are often within ourselves.

The lesser Jihad refers to the external struggle, sometimes involving physical conflict, but only in the defence of justice and against oppression. Even then, the Quran sets strict ethical guidelines. Quran 22:39 permits fighting only in cases of self-defence : "Permission [to fight] has been given to those who are being fought, because they were wronged. And indeed, Allah is competent to give them victory."

In the modern world, many people are engaged in battles for justice, whether it is against systemic racism, political oppression, or social inequality. The Quran's teachings on Jihad remind us that these struggles must be undertaken with integrity and restraint, always seeking peaceful solutions where possible and resorting to physical conflict only as a last resort.

Patience in the Modern World: An Essential Virtue

"O you who have believed, persevere and endure and remain stationed and fear Allah that you may be successful."
— (Quran 3:200)

In today's fast-paced world, patience is often seen as a sign of weakness or passivity. We live in a society that glorifies quick action and immediate results, where waiting is considered inefficient. However, the Quran's emphasis on patience is more relevant than ever, reminding us that not all things can be rushed, and that sometimes, the greatest strength lies in waiting.

Take, for instance, the global fight for climate justice. It is a slow and arduous process, requiring the patience to deal with bureaucratic red tape, public apathy, and political resistance. Activists around the world, much like the prophets in their own times, continue to advocate for change, often seeing little immediate result. Yet, they persevere, driven by the belief that their patience and persistence will eventually lead to a better world.

In personal life, too, patience can lead to unexpected blessings. Whether it's waiting for a relationship to heal, enduring a period of unemployment, or recovering from illness, the Quran teaches that those who wait with faith and patience will ultimately be rewarded. Quran 3:200 encourages believers: "O you who have believed, persevere and endure and remain stationed and fear Allah that you may be successful."

Divine Assistance: God's Help in Times of Struggle

"Indeed, I will reinforce you with a thousand from the angels, following one another."
— (Quran 8:9)

The Quran assures us that when we endure with patience and faith, we are never alone in our struggle. Quran 8:9 recounts how, during the Battle of Badr, Allah sent angels to assist the believers: "[Remember] when you asked help of your Lord, and He answered you, 'Indeed, I will reinforce you with a thousand from the angels, following one another.'" This divine intervention reminds us that, while we may feel isolated in our struggles, Allah is always with those who fight for justice and righteousness.

In modern times, divine assistance may not manifest as angels descending from the heavens, but many believers feel Allah's presence in more subtle ways. It could be an unexpected solution to a problem, a sudden moment of clarity, or the support of others at just the right time. The Quran teaches that Allah's help is always near for those who are patient and persevere.

I recall a time when I was overwhelmed by a personal crisis, feeling lost and without direction. I turned to prayer, asking for guidance and strength. Shortly after, a mentor I hadn't spoken to in years reached out to offer advice and support. This timely intervention felt like a direct response to my prayers, reminding me that Allah's assistance often comes in the form of people and opportunities that help us through our struggles.

Conclusion: The Power of Patience and Faith in the Face of Adversity

"The Lord will fight for you; you need only to be still."
— (Exodus 14:14)

The Quran provides a powerful framework for understanding how to face life's struggles. It teaches that not every fight is ours to engage in, and that sometimes, the greatest strength lies in patience and faith. Whether it's through the story of Prophet Yusuf enduring injustice or the Quran's guidance on Jihad, we learn that both internal and external battles must be approached with integrity, restraint, and an unwavering trust in Allah's plan.

In a world that often glorifies immediate action and visible results, the Quran's call to patience and faith offers a timeless reminder. By choosing to endure hardship with grace, engaging in the inner struggle to overcome our own egos, and trusting in Allah's justice, we find a strength that transcends human limitations.

Ultimately, the Quran reassures us that those who endure with patience are never truly alone. When we align our struggles with righteousness and justice, divine assistance is always near. And sometimes, the greatest victory is not in overcoming the struggle but in enduring it with unwavering faith.

5

Lord Rama's Fight for Justice and Righteousness

The Role of Dharma in Life's Battles

"Do not be overcome by evil, but overcome evil with good."
— (Romans 12:21)

In the Ramayana, one of the oldest and most revered epics in Hindu literature, the concept of Dharma (righteous duty) plays a central role. The story revolves around Lord Rama, an incarnation of the god Vishnu, who is portrayed as the ideal man, ruler, and warrior. Rama's life and the battles he fights are not just physical but are deeply rooted in the spiritual and moral principles of Dharma—righteousness and duty.

The Ramayana teaches us that life's battles, whether personal or communal, should always be fought for the sake of justice, truth, and order, not for personal gain or out of selfish desire. As Lord Rama faces his trials, he consistently chooses the path of righteousness, even when it costs him his personal happiness.

This theme resonates deeply with the biblical teachings on righteousness and justice. In Micah 6:8, the Bible says, "He has told you, O mortal, what is good; and what does the Lord require of you but to do justice, and to love kindness, and to walk humbly with your God?" Like Lord Rama, the Bible calls us to act justly and follow God's path of righteousness, regardless of personal cost.

I remember a time when I was faced with a moral dilemma at my workplace. I had to choose between speaking out against an unfair policy that was benefiting me personally or staying silent to protect my position. Inspired by the example of Lord Rama and guided by Micah 6:8, I chose to speak out, risking my own comfort for the sake of justice. Although it cost me initially, the peace I found in knowing I did the right thing was invaluable. It taught me that when we stand up for righteousness, we align ourselves with a higher purpose, even when the path is difficult.

Rama's Exile: A Test of Integrity and Duty

> *"Indeed, all who want to live a godly*
> *life in Christ Jesus will be persecuted."*
> *— (2 Timothy 3:12)*

One of the most poignant moments in the Ramayana is Lord Rama's exile into the forest for fourteen years. Just as he is about to be crowned king, his stepmother

Kaikeyi demands that he be exiled, fulfilling a promise made by her husband, King Dasharatha. Rather than resist or challenge this unjust demand, Rama accepts his fate with grace and humility, recognising that it is his duty to honour his father's word and uphold the family's honour.

Rama's exile represents a profound test of integrity. Despite being wronged, he chooses to follow his Dharma, putting the kingdom's moral order above his personal desires. His response reflects a deep understanding of righteousness—sometimes, the battles we face are not about winning but about standing firm in what is right, even when it requires personal sacrifice.

This mirrors the biblical story of Joseph, who was unjustly sold into slavery by his brothers. Rather than become bitter or seek revenge, Joseph trusted in God's plan, even during his years of suffering. Genesis 50:20 highlights Joseph's perspective on his trials: "Even though you intended to do harm to me, God intended it for good, in order to preserve a numerous people, as He is doing today." Like Rama, Joseph saw his personal struggle as part of a larger plan for justice and goodness.

In today's world, we are often faced with situations where we must choose between personal gain and doing what is right. Whether in our careers, relationships, or public life, the story of Rama's exile teaches us that true righteousness requires us to sacrifice our personal interests for the sake of duty and justice.

I once faced a similar dilemma when I was asked to endorse a decision that would benefit me financially but was ethically questionable. Like Rama, I had to choose between personal benefit and doing what was morally right. Though it was difficult, I chose to stand by my principles, and while the immediate rewards were lost, I found peace in knowing that I had followed my duty. This experience taught me that integrity is not about the rewards we receive but about the peace we gain from doing what is right.

The Battle with Ravana: Fighting for Righteousness, Not Revenge

"Beloved, never avenge yourselves, but leave room for the wrath of God; for it is written,
'Vengeance is mine, I will repay, says the Lord.'"
—(Romans 12:19)

One of the most iconic moments in the Ramayana is the epic battle between Lord Rama and Ravana, the demon king of Lanka. Ravana abducts Sita, Rama's wife, setting the stage for a war between good and evil. However, Rama's fight against Ravana is not motivated by personal vengeance, but by his duty to restore Dharma and protect his wife. The battle symbolizes the larger struggle between righteousness (Dharma) and unrighteousness (Adharma).

Rama's battle with Ravana is not merely a personal vendetta. He fights to restore order and justice in the world. His actions are not driven by hatred or anger but by the understanding that as a leader and protector, it is his duty to vanquish evil and safeguard the innocent. In Bhagavad Gita 18:47, the Gita teaches, "It is better to live your own Dharma imperfectly than to fulfil the Dharma of another with perfection." Rama embodies this principle—he knows that it is his duty to fight, and he does so with unwavering commitment to righteousness.

Similarly, the Bible teaches that the fight for righteousness should never be motivated by personal revenge or anger. Romans 12:19 says, "Beloved, never avenge yourselves, but leave room for the wrath of God; for it is written, 'Vengeance is mine, I will repay, says the Lord.'" In both the Ramayana and the Bible, we see that the battle for justice is not about seeking personal retribution but about fulfilling a higher purpose.

In modern-day struggles, this is a powerful lesson. Whether we are advocating for justice in our communities, standing up against corruption, or defending those who cannot defend themselves, we must be motivated by a desire to uphold righteousness, not by personal anger or vengeance.

I experienced this first hand when I was wronged by a close friend in a business deal. The hurt and betrayal made me want to fight back and seek justice on my own terms. But as I reflected on the stories of Rama and Jesus, I realized that my battle wasn't about seeking revenge but about doing what was right. By letting go of personal vengeance and focusing on righteousness, I was able to resolve the conflict in a way that restored peace without escalating the hurt.

Sita's Abduction: The Fight for the Protection of the Innocent

"Speak out for those who cannot speak, for the rights of all the destitute. Speak out, judge righteously, defend the rights of the poor and needy."
— (Proverbs 31:8-9)

The abduction of Sita by Ravana is a pivotal moment in the Ramayana, as it sets the stage for Rama's battle to rescue her. Sita represents innocence, purity, and virtue, and her abduction symbolizes the violation of these values. Rama's mission to rescue Sita is not just about reclaiming his wife but about restoring justice and protecting the innocent.

This theme of protecting the innocent is echoed throughout the Bible as well. In Proverbs 31:8-9, scripture urges us, "Speak out for those who cannot speak, for the rights of all the destitute. Speak out, judge righteously, defend the rights of the poor and needy." Just as Rama fights to rescue Sita, the Bible calls us to defend the vulnerable and stand up for those who are oppressed.

In today's world, we see the fight for the protection of the innocent in many forms. Whether it's advocating for the rights of the unborn, fighting against human trafficking, or working to end poverty, the call to protect the vulnerable remains central to both the Ramayana and the Bible.

I've seen this in my own life through the work of non-profit organisations that fight against child exploitation. One organisation I volunteered with worked tirelessly to rescue children from trafficking and provide them with safe environments. Their mission reminded me of the story of Sita and Rama—the fight to protect the innocent is one of the most righteous battles we can engage in, and it requires perseverance, courage, and unwavering faith.

Present-Day Realities: The Struggle for Justice and Righteous Leadership

"When the righteous are in authority, the people rejoice; but when the wicked rule, the people groan."
— (Proverbs 29:2)

The story of Lord Rama's journey in the Ramayana offers profound lessons for today's world, particularly in the context of leadership and justice. Rama is depicted as the ideal king, whose rule is marked by fairness, compassion, and a deep commitment to the well-being of his people. His story calls into question the qualities we value in leaders today.

In a world where leadership is often driven by personal gain, corruption, or power, Rama's example stands as a model for righteous leadership. His life reminds us that true leaders are those who prioritise the well-being of others, who act with integrity, and who fight for justice, even when it comes at a personal cost.

The Bible echoes these principles of righteous leadership. Proverbs 29:2 says, "When the righteous are in authority, the people rejoice; but when the wicked rule, the people groan." Both the Ramayana and the Bible teach that leadership grounded in justice and righteousness leads to peace and prosperity, while corrupt leadership brings suffering and disorder.

In the modern world, the fight for righteous leadership is more important than ever. Whether in politics, business, or religious institutions, we need leaders who, like Rama, prioritise justice and act with moral integrity. This is not just a battle for power, but a battle for the soul of our societies, one that requires each of us to engage with discernment and dedication to righteousness.

Conclusion: The Path of Righteousness Requires Sacrifice and Faith

> *"But strive first for the kingdom of God and His righteousness, and all these things will be given to you as well."*
> *— (Matthew 6:33)*

The Ramayana teaches us that the path of righteousness is not an easy one. Lord Rama's journey is filled with trials, sacrifices, and moral dilemmas, but through it all, he remains committed to his Dharma. Like Rama, we are called to fight for justice and righteousness, even when it requires personal sacrifice or when the path ahead seems unclear.

In the Bible, the call to pursue righteousness is central to our relationship with God. Matthew 6:33 says, "But strive first for the kingdom of God and His righteousness, and all these things will be given to you as well." Both the Ramayana and the Bible affirm that when we seek God's righteousness, we are supported in ways that transcend our understanding.

The stories of Lord Rama's exile, his battle with Ravana, and his unwavering commitment to protecting the innocent remind us that righteousness often comes at a cost. Yet, it is a cost worth paying, for it aligns us with a higher purpose and a deeper peace. As we navigate our own battles for justice and truth, may we be inspired by the example of Lord Rama and the teachings of the Bible to fight not for ourselves, but for the greater good, trusting that in the end, righteousness will prevail.

6

The Struggle for Justice and Righteous Leadership

The Call to Righteous Leadership

"When the righteous are in authority, the people rejoice; but when the wicked rule, the people groan."
— (Proverbs 29:2)

Throughout the Bible, righteous leadership is portrayed as essential to the health and prosperity of a people or nation. God repeatedly calls leaders to act with integrity, wisdom, and justice. Leadership in the biblical sense is not about personal glory, power, or control but about service, humility, and righteousness. Proverbs 29:2 illustrates this perfectly: "When the righteous are in authority, the people rejoice; but when the wicked rule, the people groan."

In the Bible, leadership is a burden that requires responsibility, sacrifice, and a commitment to doing what is right in the eyes of God. Leaders are tasked with safeguarding justice, protecting the vulnerable, and guiding their people toward righteousness. This is why God repeatedly raises up righteous leaders, such as Moses, Joshua, and David, to lead His people through times of trial and crisis.

I have witnessed the power of righteous leadership in action, particularly within my church community. During a time of division and uncertainty, our pastor, who led with integrity, humility, and wisdom, guided us through these difficult times. He did not lead for personal gain but to fulfil his duty to God and the congregation. His example reflected the teachings of Jesus, who said, "The greatest among you will be your servant" (Matthew 23:11). True leadership, as the Bible teaches, is about service, not power.

In today's world, this lesson is crucial. Whether in politics, business, or religious institutions, we see the impact of corrupt leadership—leaders who put personal ambition above the needs of the people they serve. The Bible's call to righteous leadership is a reminder that leaders must act with justice and humility, seeking the good of others above all.

Moses: Leading with Justice and Humility

"Now the man Moses was very humble, more so than anyone else on the face of the earth."
— *(Numbers 12:3)*

One of the most profound examples of righteous leadership in the Bible is Moses. Chosen by God to lead the Israelites out of slavery in Egypt, Moses embodies the qualities of a leader who seeks justice and righteousness above all else. Moses is described as a humble servant of God, reluctant to take on the role of leader at first, yet fully committed to carrying out God's will. Numbers 12:3 says, "Now the man Moses was very humble, more so than anyone else on the face of the earth."

Moses' leadership was marked by his desire to ensure justice for the Israelites. He constantly interceded with God on behalf of the people, even when they rebelled against him. One of the most powerful moments in Moses' leadership journey occurs in Exodus 32, when the Israelites build the golden calf. God's anger burns against them, and He considers destroying them. But Moses, despite the people's disobedience, pleads for their forgiveness and asks God to spare them. His intercession shows his deep commitment to justice and mercy, even for a wayward people.

Moses' story teaches us that righteous leadership requires humility and a heart for justice. He did not seek power for himself but acted as a servant of God, guiding the Israelites with patience and perseverance. The justice he sought was not rooted in human law but in the divine law that God revealed to him on Mount Sinai—the Ten Commandments. These commandments laid the foundation for justice, equity, and moral order, which Moses worked tirelessly to uphold.

In my personal life, I've often reflected on Moses' humility and the way he led with both strength and compassion. As a leader in a community group, I've found that leading with humility—listening to others, seeking their well-being, and standing for what is right even when it's difficult—brings about unity and trust. Moses' example reminds us that true leadership is not about asserting control but about serving others faithfully.

David: The Imperfect but Righteous King

"And David shepherded them with integrity of heart; with skilful hands he led them."
— (Psalm 78:72)

King David is another example of righteous leadership in the Bible, though his journey was far from perfect. Chosen by God to be king of Israel, David is described as a man after God's own heart (1 Samuel 13:14). Though he made mistakes—most notably in his sin with Bathsheba and the subsequent cover-up—David's overall commitment to righteousness and justice marked his reign.

David's leadership was deeply rooted in his relationship with God. As a shepherd-king, he understood that his role was to care for the people of Israel as a shepherd cares for his flock. Psalm 78:72 describes David's leadership: "And David shepherded them with integrity of heart; with skilful hands he led them." Despite his human flaws, David consistently sought God's guidance and repented when he sinned, demonstrating that righteous leadership includes acknowledging mistakes and seeking forgiveness.

One of the most powerful demonstrations of David's commitment to righteousness comes in his refusal to harm King Saul, even though Saul was trying to kill de him. Twice, David had the opportunity to kill Saul and take the throne, but both times he refrained, saying, "The Lord forbid that I should do this thing to my lord, the Lord's anointed, to raise my hand against him" (1 Samuel 24:6). David knew that the path to leadership and justice must be aligned with God's will and timing, not through personal ambition or violence.

David's story is a powerful reminder that righteous leadership does not require perfection, but it does require a heart that continually seeks God's will. Even when we fall short, as David did, we can still pursue righteousness by turning back to God in repentance and striving to lead with integrity.

In modern leadership contexts, this lesson is invaluable. Leaders today are often pressured to maintain an image of perfection, but the Bible teaches that righteous leadership is about humility, repentance, and a genuine commitment to justice and truth. I've seen this in my work with community leaders, where those who acknowledge their mistakes and seek reconciliation are often the ones who build the strongest, most trustworthy teams.

Jesus: The Model of Servant Leadership

> *"Whoever wants to be first must be last of all and servant of all."*
> *— (Mark 9:35)*

The ultimate example of righteous leadership in the Bible is Jesus Christ. His leadership was defined not by power or authority but by servanthood, sacrifice, and an unwavering commitment to truth and justice. Matthew 20:28 says, "Just as the Son of Man came not to be served but to serve, and to give His life a ransom for many."

Jesus' leadership was radical in its emphasis on serving others. He washed His disciples' feet, healed the sick, and ministered to the outcasts of society. In doing so, He demonstrated that true leadership is not about elevating oneself but about lifting others up. Jesus' entire ministry was focused on justice for the marginalised, love for the unlovable, and compassion for the suffering.

One of the most powerful examples of Jesus' leadership is His response to the Pharisees and religious leaders who were more concerned with legalism than with justice and mercy. Matthew 23:23 records Jesus' rebuke of the religious elite: "Woe to you, scribes and Pharisees, hypocrites! For you tithe mint, dill, and cumin, and have neglected the weightier matters of the law: justice and mercy and faith. It is these you ought to have practiced without neglecting the others." Jesus called out the hypocrisy of those in positions of power, reminding them that leadership is not about adhering to empty rituals but about seeking justice, showing mercy, and being faithful to God's truth.

Jesus' leadership culminated in His ultimate sacrifice on the cross, where He gave His life for the redemption of humanity. This act of sacrificial love defines the very essence of righteous leadership—putting others before oneself, even to the point of death. John 15:13 reflects this: "No one has greater love than this, to lay down one's life for one's friends."

As believers, we are called to follow Jesus' example of servant leadership. Whether in our families, workplaces, or communities, we are to lead with humility, compassion, and a commitment to justice, always seeking to serve rather than to be served.

I've tried to live out this example of servant leadership in my own life, particularly in mentoring younger colleagues. Instead of using my position to exert control or assert authority, I strive to lead by example, offering guidance, support, and encouragement. Like Jesus, I aim to lift others up, helping them grow in their own paths. The Bible's teaching on servant leadership has been a guiding principle in my relationships and work, reminding me that the most powerful form of leadership is one rooted in love and service.

The Fight for Justice: A Constant Battle

> *"But let justice roll down like waters, and righteousness like an ever-flowing stream."*
> *— (Amos 5:24)*

In both the Old and New Testaments, the Bible speaks of the ongoing struggle for justice. The prophet Amos 5:24 declares, "But let justice roll down like waters, and righteousness like an ever-flowing stream!" This powerful imagery reminds us that justice is not a one-time event but an ongoing pursuit. Righteous leadership requires a continual commitment to seek justice for the oppressed, the marginalised, and the vulnerable.

In the modern world, this struggle for justice is as relevant as ever. We see injustice in the form of systemic racism, economic inequality, and social injustice. The Bible calls us, as followers of Christ, to stand up against these injustices and to work toward a society that reflects God's heart for righteousness.

A powerful modern example of the biblical call for justice is the Civil Rights Movement led by Dr. Martin Luther King Jr. Rooted in his Christian faith, Dr. King's leadership was guided by biblical principles of justice, equality, and nonviolence. He often drew upon scripture to rally people to the cause of justice, famously quoting Amos 5:24 in his speeches. Dr. King's fight for justice mirrors the biblical call for leaders to speak truth to power and to advocate for the marginalised.

In my own community, I've seen local leaders step up to fight for justice in various ways—whether it's advocating for the homeless, working to improve education for underprivileged children, or addressing issues of racial inequality. These modern-day leaders embody the biblical call to righteousness and justice, reminding us that the fight for justice is ongoing and requires dedication, courage, and faith.

Conclusion: Righteous Leadership Requires Sacrifice and Faithfulness

"Learn to do good; seek justice, rescue the oppressed, defend the orphan, plead for the widow."
— *(Isaiah 1:17)*

The Bible presents a clear picture of what it means to be a righteous leader: one who serves others, seeks justice, and walks humbly with God. From Moses' humility to David's repentance, from Jesus' servant leadership to the prophetic call for justice, the Bible teaches us that true leadership is not about power or prestige but about righteousness, sacrifice, and faithfulness to God's will.

As we navigate the complexities of leadership in today's world—whether in our homes, workplaces, churches, or communities—we are called to follow the biblical model of righteous leadership. This means standing up for justice, serving others selflessly, and leading with integrity and humility. The struggle for justice and righteousness is not easy, but with God's guidance, we can be leaders who reflect His heart and bring His justice to a broken world.

As Isaiah 1:17 exhorts us, "Learn to do good; seek justice, rescue the oppressed, defend the orphan, plead for the widow." Let us take up the call to lead with righteousness, trusting that God will guide us in every battle we face.

7

Enduring Suffering with Hope and Conviction

The Nature of Suffering in the Christian Life

"We also boast in our sufferings, knowing that suffering produces endurance, and endurance produces character, and character produces hope."
— (Romans 5:3-4)

Suffering is a universal human experience, but the Bible teaches that suffering, when endured with faith, can lead to spiritual growth and deeper intimacy with God. Throughout scripture, we see examples of God's people facing trials and tribulations, yet holding on to hope and conviction. The Bible does not promise a life free from suffering, but it does offer the assurance that God is present in our pain, working to bring about His good purposes. Romans 5:3-4 says, "We also boast in our sufferings, knowing that suffering produces endurance, and endurance produces character, and character produces hope."

Suffering, from a biblical perspective, is not meaningless. It refines us, shapes our character, and draws us closer to God. The Bible teaches that enduring hardship with hope transforms us into people of resilience and faith, much like gold refined by fire. This transformation is evident in the lives of many biblical figures who faced tremendous suffering, yet emerged stronger in their faith.

Personally, I have walked through seasons of deep suffering—times of loss, illness, and emotional pain. But in those moments, it was often the assurance of God's presence that sustained me. Isaiah 43:2 became a verse I clung to: "When you pass through the waters, I will be with you; and through the rivers, they shall not overwhelm you; when you walk through fire you shall not be burned, and the flame shall not consume you." This promise reminded me that even in the darkest times, God walks with us, and that gave me the strength to endure.

The Story of Job: Unwavering Faith Amid Unbearable Loss

> *"The Lord gave, and the Lord has taken away; blessed be the name of the Lord."— (Job 1:21)*

The story of Job is perhaps the most famous biblical example of enduring suffering with faith. Job was a righteous man, yet he lost everything—his wealth, his children, his health—in a series of devastating events. Despite his immense suffering, Job refused to curse God or abandon his faith. Instead, he lamented, questioned, and sought understanding from God, all while holding onto his belief that God was just, even when he couldn't see it.

Job's perseverance is captured in Job 1:21, where he declares, "The Lord gave, and the Lord has taken away; blessed be the name of the Lord." This powerful statement reflects a deep trust in God's sovereignty. Though Job did not understand why he was suffering, he continued to believe that God's purposes were good.

Job's story reminds us that suffering is not always a result of wrongdoing. Sometimes, righteous people suffer, and the reasons may remain beyond human understanding. But what makes Job's response so remarkable is his unwavering conviction that God remained faithful, even when life seemed unbearably cruel. In the end, God restored Job's fortunes, but more importantly, Job's faith had deepened through his trial.

In my own life, I've faced situations that seemed to have no reason or purpose—times when I wondered why God was allowing such hardship. Like Job, I questioned, wrestled, and sought answers. But through prayer and reflection, I began to understand that sometimes, suffering is not for us to explain, but to endure with faith. I learned that even when answers are elusive, God's presence is a comfort, and trusting Him through suffering can lead to greater spiritual depth.

Paul: Suffering for the Gospel

> *"My grace is sufficient for you, for*
> *power is made perfect in weakness."*
> *— (2 Corinthians 12:9)*

The Apostle Paul provides another powerful example of enduring suffering with hope and conviction. Throughout his ministry, Paul faced persecution, imprisonment, beatings, and countless hardships. Yet, he viewed his suffering not as a reason for despair but as a way to glorify Christ and advance the gospel. 2 Corinthians 12:9-10 captures Paul's perspective on suffering: "But He said to me, 'My grace is sufficient for you, for power is made perfect in weakness.' So, I will boast all the more gladly of my weaknesses, so that the power of Christ may dwell in me."

Paul's life teaches us that suffering can be a way for God's grace and power to be revealed in our lives. Rather than seeking to escape his suffering, Paul embraced it, believing that in his weakness, Christ's strength was made visible. His perseverance through suffering became a testimony of faith, inspiring countless believers throughout history.

In Philippians 1:12, Paul writes, "I want you to know, beloved, that what has happened to me has actually helped to spread the gospel." Here, Paul reflects on his imprisonment, viewing it not as a setback but as an opportunity for God's work to be accomplished. Paul's perspective is a powerful reminder that God can use our suffering for His purposes, even when we cannot see the full picture.

I've often found encouragement in Paul's words when facing trials. One particular season of my life involved a prolonged period of financial difficulty, and it was hard to see how anything good could come of it. But as I leaned on God's grace and continued to serve Him despite my circumstances, I saw how that season allowed me to develop deeper compassion for others going through similar struggles. Paul's example taught me that, like him, we can endure suffering with conviction, trusting that God is using our pain for His greater purposes.

Jesus: The Ultimate Example of Suffering for the Greater Good

"Looking to Jesus the pioneer and perfecter of our faith, who for the sake of the joy that was set before Him endured the cross, disregarding its shame, and has taken His seat at the right hand of the throne of God."
— (Hebrews 12:2)

The ultimate example of enduring suffering for the sake of a greater purpose is found in Jesus Christ. His entire ministry led to the cross, where He willingly endured unimaginable physical and emotional suffering to accomplish the redemption of humanity. Isaiah 53:3 prophesied Jesus as the "man of sorrows, and acquainted with grief," and indeed, Jesus' suffering was unparalleled. Yet, He chose to endure it out of love and obedience to the Father.

In Hebrews 12:2, we are reminded of the mindset with which Jesus approached His suffering: "Looking to Jesus the pioneer and perfecter of our faith, who for the sake of the joy that was set before Him endured the cross, disregarding its shame, and has taken His seat at the right hand of the throne of God." Jesus looked beyond the immediate pain of the cross to the joy of what it would accomplish—the salvation of the world.

As Christians, we are called to take up our own crosses and follow Jesus, enduring suffering for the sake of the gospel. Matthew 16:24 says, "Then Jesus told His disciples, 'If any want to become my followers, let them deny themselves and take up their cross and follow me.'" This does not mean that we seek suffering, but that we are willing to endure it when it comes, trusting that God will use it for a greater good.

In my personal journey, there have been times when following Christ led to loss or hardship—whether it was standing up for my faith in an environment where it was unwelcome, or making sacrifices for the sake of serving others. Yet, in those moments of difficulty, I found comfort in Jesus' example. His willingness to endure suffering for the sake of love inspires me to continue the path of faith, knowing that whatever trials I face, they are part of a larger story of redemption.

Present-Day Realities: Suffering with Conviction in a World of Uncertainty

*"Cast all your anxiety on Him,
because He cares for you."*
— *(1 Peter 5:7)*

Today's world is marked by uncertainty, injustice, and suffering on many levels—whether through personal loss, global crises, or societal upheaval. The Bible's teachings on suffering with hope and conviction are more relevant than ever. While we live in a culture that often seeks to avoid or numb pain, scripture encourages us to face suffering head-on, trusting in God's presence and promises.

One powerful modern example of enduring suffering with hope is the life of Nelson Mandela, who spent 27 years in prison for his stand against apartheid in South Africa. Despite his immense suffering, Mandela emerged from prison with a spirit of reconciliation, believing that his suffering had a purpose and that justice would ultimately prevail. His life, much like the stories of Job and Paul, demonstrates that suffering can lead to transformation, both personally and collectively.

I've also seen this principle at work in local communities, particularly in the lives of individuals who have endured immense hardship—whether it's illness, financial loss, or personal betrayal. Yet, through their faith, they've come out of those seasons with a deeper understanding of God's faithfulness. Their stories remind me that while suffering is inevitable, how we respond to it can be a testimony of God's grace and strength.

The Promise of Eternal Glory: Hope Beyond Suffering

"For this slight momentary affliction is preparing us for an eternal weight of glory beyond all measure."
— (2 Corinthians 4:17)

The Bible offers the ultimate promise for those who endure suffering with faith—the hope of eternal glory. 2 Corinthians 4:17 provides a powerful perspective on suffering: "For this slight momentary affliction is preparing us for an eternal weight of glory beyond all measure." This verse reminds us that no matter how difficult our present sufferings may be, they are temporary compared to the eternal joy that awaits us in the presence of God.

In Romans 8:18, Paul also reflects on this future hope: "I consider that the sufferings of this present time are not worth comparing with the glory about to be revealed to us." This eternal perspective gives believers the strength to endure suffering, knowing that God's ultimate plan includes not only redemption but also a future free from pain, sorrow, and death.

In my darkest moments, this promise of eternal glory has been a source of great comfort. The knowledge that one day, all suffering will be wiped away gives me the hope to press on, even when life feels overwhelming. It's a reminder that the struggles of this world are temporary and that God's final victory is one of restoration and joy.

Conclusion: Suffering with Hope, Conviction, and Faith

"Blessed is anyone who endures temptation. Such a one has stood the test and will receive the crown of life that the Lord has promised to those who love Him."
— (James 1:12)

The Bible teaches us that suffering, though painful, is not without purpose. Whether it's Job's steadfastness in the face of loss, Paul's endurance through persecution, or Jesus' ultimate sacrifice on the cross, we see that suffering can lead to greater spiritual growth, deeper faith, and a testimony of God's grace. By enduring suffering with hope and conviction, we participate in God's larger story of redemption.

As we face the inevitable trials of life—whether they come in the form of personal hardship, societal challenges, or global crises—we can take comfort in the fact that God is with us, working all things for our good. James 1:12 says, "Blessed is anyone who endures temptation. Such a one has stood the test and will receive the crown of life that the Lord has promised to those who love Him." With this assurance, we can endure suffering with faith, knowing that God is faithful and that one day, all suffering will be transformed into eternal glory.

8

The Mahabharata – The Complexity of Battle and Moral Dilemmas

The Mahabharata: A Mirror of Life's Moral Complexities

"The battle between good and evil is waged within every human heart."
— *(Fyodor Dostoevsky)*

The Mahabharata is a grand and intricate epic that portrays the complexities of human life, moral choices, and the struggle between righteousness and unrighteousness. Unlike simple narratives of good versus evil, the Mahabharata is a deeply philosophical text that reflects the moral dilemmas and struggles faced by individuals in times of conflict. Through its characters and their stories, the Mahabharata teaches profound lessons on Dharma (righteous duty), justice, loyalty, and the consequences of actions.

This epic is not just a story of war but a profound exploration of the human condition. It presents a nuanced view of morality, showing that life's battles are seldom black and white. The choices made by its characters are fraught with complexity, reflecting the intricate web of duty, relationships, and moral responsibility that all of us navigate in our lives. In this sense, the Mahabharata serves as a mirror, reflecting the struggles we all face in upholding what is right amidst the grey areas of life.

The Role of Krishna: Guiding the Pandavas to Fight for Justice and Righteousness

> *"When you have to choose between two evils, choose the one you've never tried before."*
> — *(Mae West)*

One of the most pivotal aspects of the Mahabharata is the guidance of Lord Krishna, who serves as both a divine counsellor and charioteer to Arjuna. Krishna's wisdom is essential to understanding the moral and spiritual underpinnings of the Kurukshetra War. His teachings, encapsulated in the Bhagavad Gita, guide the Pandavas, particularly Arjuna, through their moral conflicts.

Arjuna, the mightiest warrior of the Pandavas, is paralysed by a deep moral dilemma on the battlefield. As he stands on the threshold of war, he is filled with doubt and sorrow, overwhelmed by the thought of killing his own family members, teachers, and friends. He questions the righteousness of engaging in such a destructive battle. Arjuna's inner conflict represents the struggle many of us face when we must choose between our personal emotions and our moral obligations.

In response, Krishna delivers the teachings of the Bhagavad Gita, emphasising the importance of Dharma and righteous action. Bhagavad Gita 2:31 highlights Krishna's counsel to Arjuna: "Considering your dharma, you should not waver. For a warrior, nothing is more honourable than a war against evil." Krishna reminds Arjuna that his duty as a warrior is to fight for justice, regardless of personal ties or emotional attachments.

Krishna's teachings in the Gita reveal a profound truth: righteousness must guide our actions, even when the path is difficult. In today's world, we are often confronted with moral dilemmas, where the right decision may come at a personal cost. Krishna's wisdom encourages us to focus on our duty and the greater good, even when we feel uncertain or conflicted.

Personally, I have often grappled with making tough decisions where family loyalties or personal emotions were at odds with what was morally right. Krishna's counsel to Arjuna—detachment from the results and commitment to Dharma—has been a source of inspiration for me. It has taught me that the pursuit of justice and righteousness must come first, and that personal suffering or loss is secondary to fulfilling one's moral obligations.

Bhishma's Vow: A Fight for Loyalty and Honour That Brought Personal Struggle

> *"It is not what we give up, but what we do not accept that defines who we are."*
> — *(Sylvain Reynard)*

One of the most tragic and complex figures in the Mahabharata is Bhishma, a man whose life is shaped by a vow he took early on, which ultimately becomes the source of his inner conflict and suffering. Bhishma's story is one of personal sacrifice, as he prioritises loyalty and honour over his own desires and even his understanding of righteousness.

Bhishma, born as the son of King Shantanu, takes a vow of celibacy and renounces his claim to the throne to ensure that his father's love interest, Satyavati, and her descendants would rule Hastinapuram. His vow of lifelong loyalty to the throne binds him to serve as a protector of the kingdom, no matter who sits on the throne.

As the Mahabharata unfolds, Bhishma finds himself fighting for the Kauravas, despite knowing that their cause is unjust. His loyalty to the throne and his vow prevents him from switching sides, even though his conscience tells him that the Pandavas are on the side of Dharma. Bhishma's inner turmoil highlights the complexity of Dharma, where loyalty, duty, and righteousness often conflict with one another.

Bhishma's story teaches us that personal vows and commitments, while noble, can sometimes lead to moral dilemmas. It reflects the tension between loyalty to one's word and the pursuit of justice. Bhagavad Gita 18:47 touches on this complexity: "It is better to perform one's own dharma imperfectly than to perform another's perfectly." Bhishma's struggle is a reminder that the path of righteousness is often fraught with difficult choices, and sometimes, even the most honourable intentions can lead to suffering.

In today's context, Bhishma's story can be seen in those who are bound by duty to organisations, governments, or traditions, even when they recognise that those institutions may be flawed or unjust. I have seen this conflict play out in my own life, where individuals remain loyal to commitments out of a sense of duty, even when those commitments clash with their moral compass. Bhishma's life is a reminder that even loyalty and honour can lead to inner conflict if they are not aligned with righteousness.

Draupadi's Humiliation: A Woman's Fight for Dignity and Justice

"When we speak, we are afraid our words will not be heard or welcomed. But when we are silent, we are still afraid. So, it is better to speak."
— Audre Lorde

One of the most powerful and heartbreaking moments in the Mahabharata is the public humiliation of Draupadi, the wife of the Pandavas, during the infamous dice game. Draupadi is not only a central figure in the epic but also a symbol of justice, dignity, and resilience in the face of immense personal suffering.

In a fateful game of dice, Yudhishthira, the eldest Pandava, loses everything, including his brothers and himself, to the Kauravas. In a final, desperate gamble, he wagers Draupadi, and she is subsequently dragged into the court, where she is publicly humiliated. The Kaurava prince Dushasana attempts to disrobe her, but in a moment of divine intervention, Draupadi's honour is preserved by Krishna, who ensures that her sari becomes endless, preventing her disrobing.

This moment of humiliation becomes a turning point in the epic, as Draupadi demands justice for the wrongs done to her. Her dignity violated, Draupadi questions the elders in the court, asking if any of them will stand up for justice. When they remain silent, it is Krishna who steps in as her protector, ensuring that her dignity is restored.

Draupadi's fight for justice is not just about personal revenge—it is about upholding the principles of Dharma. Her ordeal highlights the vulnerability of women in patriarchal societies and the importance of divine justice when human institutions fail. Draupadi's courage in standing up for her dignity resonates with the fight for justice faced by many women throughout history and today.

In many ways, Draupadi's story reminds me of Psalm 9:9, which says, "The Lord is a stronghold for the oppressed, a stronghold in times of trouble." Like Draupadi, many individuals today face humiliation and injustice, and they must turn to their faith for strength. Draupadi's resilience and her refusal to accept injustice without protest serve as a powerful example of the fight for dignity and the role of divine intervention in times of oppression.

The Importance of Choosing Battles That Align with Dharma (Cosmic Law and Order)

> *"True peace is not merely the absence of war, it is the presence of justice."*
> — *Jane Addams*

At its core, the Mahabharata is a story about choosing the right battles—those that align with Dharma, or cosmic law and order. Throughout the epic, the characters are faced with difficult decisions, and the central question is always whether their actions are in line with Dharma.

Krishna's teachings to Arjuna during the Kurukshetra War emphasise the importance of fulfilling one's duty, regardless of personal attachments. However, the Mahabharata also shows that not all battles are worth fighting. Some battles, like Bhishma's, are born out of personal vows that conflict with righteousness, while others, like Draupadi's, are necessary to restore justice and order.

In the end, the Mahabharata teaches us that the most important battles are those that uphold Dharma, even when they are fraught with personal sacrifice and moral complexity. The war fought by the Pandavas is not for power or revenge but for the restoration of justice and the protection of the innocent.

This lesson is particularly relevant in today's world, where individuals are often faced with the choice of engaging in battles that may not serve the greater good. Whether it's in personal relationships, politics, or social justice, the Mahabharata encourages us to carefully consider which battles align with our values and the greater purpose of righteousness.

In my own life, I have found that some battles—whether in the workplace or in personal relationships—are not worth fighting if they don't align with my deeper values. The Mahabharata's emphasis on Dharma reminds me to choose my battles wisely, ensuring that they are grounded in justice and a larger purpose.

Conclusion: The Complex Nature of Moral Choices

> *"It is our choices that show what we truly are,*
> *far more than our abilities."*
> *— J.K. Rowling*

The Mahabharata is a profound exploration of the complexity of moral choices and the battles we face in life. Through the stories of Krishna, Bhishma, Draupadi, and the Pandavas, we see that the path of righteousness is not always clear-cut. It requires discernment, courage, and a deep understanding of Dharma.

As we navigate the challenges and moral dilemmas of modern life, the lessons of the Mahabharata remind us to seek justice, uphold dignity, and choose battles that align with our highest values. Whether in personal conflicts or larger societal struggles, the Mahabharata teaches us that the ultimate victory lies in the pursuit of righteousness, even when the road is fraught with difficulty.

9

The Taoism – The Power of Non-Resistance and Harmony

The Concept of Wu Wei: Acting Through Non-Action

"By letting go, it all gets done.
The world is won by those who let it go."
— *Lao Tzu*

One of the core teachings of Taoism is the concept of Wu Wei, often translated as "non-action" or "effortless action." Unlike many philosophies that emphasise forceful effort and struggle to achieve results, Taoism teaches that the most effective and harmonious way to live is to align with the natural flow of the universe, taking action that is spontaneous and unforced. Tao Te Ching 2 says, "The sage acts by doing nothing, and yet everything is done."

Wu Wei does not mean inaction or laziness, but rather acting in a way that is in harmony with the natural order of things. It's about finding balance and letting go of unnecessary effort or resistance. This principle teaches that when we cease to fight against the natural flow of life and instead move with it, we achieve more with less effort, allowing things to unfold naturally.

In my own life, I've often found that when I try to force situations—whether in relationships, work, or personal goals—I face resistance, stress, and frustration. But when I take a step back and allow things to unfold more naturally, I find that solutions emerge on their own, often better than what I could have planned. Wu Wei has taught me to trust in the process and to stop forcing outcomes that may not be aligned with the natural flow.

In the modern world, where people are constantly encouraged to "hustle" and "grind" their way to success, Taoism offers a refreshing counterbalance. It teaches us that success does not always come from excessive effort, but from aligning ourselves with the rhythms of nature, making decisions with calmness, and letting go of our obsession with control.

The Tao: Living in Harmony with the Way of the Universe

> *"Those who flow as life flows know*
> *they need no other force."*
> *— Lao Tzu*

The essence of Taoism lies in understanding the Tao, or "The Way," which refers to the fundamental principle that governs the universe. The Tao is the natural order of things, and Taoism teaches that everything in the universe flows according to the Tao, whether we realise it or not. By recognising and aligning with the Tao, we live in harmony with the world around us.

Tao Te Ching 25 describes the Tao as: "There was something formless and perfect before the universe was born. It is serene, empty, solitary, unchanging, infinite, eternally present. It is the mother of the universe. For lack of a better name, I call it the Tao."

Taoism encourages individuals to seek harmony, both within themselves and with the world around them, by accepting the natural course of events rather than resisting it. This doesn't mean passively accepting injustice or suffering, but rather finding ways to work within the natural flow of life to bring about positive change.

For example, in conflicts or challenging situations, rather than trying to force an outcome, Taoism teaches us to respond flexibly, like water. Water is soft and yielding, yet it can wear down the hardest rock over time. By adopting this mindset, we learn to navigate life's challenges with grace and resilience, finding solutions that are in harmony with the Tao rather than through brute force.

This idea resonates with many of my own experiences, particularly when facing personal and professional challenges. There have been times when I've tried to "push through" obstacles, only to find myself more frustrated and blocked. But when I step back, re-evaluate, and allow things to flow naturally, the obstacles often dissolve on their own, or I find a better way around them. Taoism has taught me that true strength lies not in resistance, but in flexibility and adaptability.

In today's fast-paced and chaotic world, the concept of living in harmony with the Tao is more relevant than ever. As we face increasing pressures to succeed, achieve, and control, Taoism reminds us to find peace in the flow of life, trusting that the universe has a natural order that we are part of.

Yin and Yang: The Balance of Opposites

> *"Without darkness, we wouldn't know*
> *the warmth of light."*
> *— Author Unknown*

Another central teaching of Taoism is the concept of Yin and Yang, the complementary forces that make up the universe. Yin represents qualities like darkness, passivity, and receptivity, while Yang represents light, activity, and dynamism. Together, they create balance and harmony in the world, as one cannot exist without the other.

Tao Te Ching 42 reflects on this duality: "The Tao gave birth to One. One gave birth to Two. Two gave birth to Three. And Three gave birth to all things. All things have their backs to the female and stand facing the male. When male and female combine, all things achieve harmony."

Yin and Yang symbolise the balance between opposing forces—light and dark, strong and weak, action and rest. Taoism teaches that life's challenges arise when we are out of balance, and the key to a harmonious life is recognising and embracing both Yin and Yang. Instead of resisting one aspect or overemphasising another, we are encouraged to seek balance and integration.

In my own life, I've noticed that when I focus too much on "Yang" activities—being busy, productive, and constantly in motion—I often feel drained and disconnected. On the other hand, when I embrace more "Yin" qualities, like rest, reflection, and openness, I regain balance and feel more at peace. Taoism reminds us that balance is not static but dynamic; it requires ongoing awareness and adjustment.

Yin and Yang are also important in understanding relationships, both personal and professional. Just as these opposing forces need each other to create harmony, so too do people with different perspectives, skills, and approaches. Taoism teaches us that diversity and difference should be celebrated, not resisted, as they are essential for creating balance and wholeness.

In today's world, where people often prioritise activity, achievement, and success (Yang), the principle of balance from Taoism invites us to slow down, reflect, and embrace the quieter, more contemplative aspects of life (Yin). This balance can lead to greater inner peace, improved relationships, and a more harmonious approach to the challenges of life.

Non-Resistance: Finding Strength in Yielding

> *"A tree that is unbending is easily broken."*
> *— Lao Tzu*

One of the most profound teachings of Taoism is the power of non-resistance. Instead of meeting challenges with force and opposition, Taoism advocates for finding strength in yielding, much like how a tree bends in the wind without breaking. Tao Te Ching 22 states, "Yield and overcome; Bend and be straight; Empty and be full; Wear out and be new; Have little and gain; Have much and be confused."

This concept of non-resistance is particularly powerful when facing adversity. Taoism teaches that resistance often leads to more conflict, whereas yielding allows us to adapt and flow with circumstances. Like water, which yields to every shape and obstacle but ultimately carves through mountains, non-resistance is not about giving up, but about finding creative and flexible ways to overcome challenges.

I have found this teaching to be especially helpful in moments of conflict or disagreement. Rather than insisting on being right or forcing my perspective, I've learned to "yield" by listening and understanding the other person's point of view. Often, this leads to a more peaceful and productive resolution than if I had tried to overpower the situation with argument or force.

In today's highly competitive and confrontational world, the idea of finding strength in yielding is a radical departure from the norm. Yet, it is often the softer, more flexible approach that leads to long-term success and harmony. Whether in personal relationships, business negotiations, or societal conflicts, Taoism's teaching of non-resistance offers a way to navigate challenges without escalating them.

Present-Day Realities: Taoism's Relevance in a Modern World

"Nature does not hurry, yet everything is accomplished."
— Lao Tzu

As we navigate the complexities of modern life—its pressures, conflicts, and uncertainties—Taoism's teachings of harmony, balance, and non-resistance provide valuable guidance. In a world that often values forceful action, constant productivity, and individual control, Taoism offers an alternative perspective: that true strength comes from flexibility, wisdom comes from stillness, and success comes from aligning with the natural flow of life.

Many of today's challenges—whether they be environmental crises, political divisions, or personal stress—can be approached from a Taoist perspective of balance and non-resistance. By recognising the natural rhythms and flows of the world, we can work with them rather than against them, finding solutions that are sustainable, peaceful, and harmonious.

For example, in the face of environmental degradation, Taoism teaches us to respect the natural world and to live in harmony with it, rather than exploiting it for short-term gains. In political conflicts, Taoism invites us to seek common ground and harmony, rather than escalating tensions through forceful rhetoric and division. And in our personal lives, Taoism reminds us that peace and fulfilments come not from constantly striving for more, but from finding balance and contentment in the present moment.

Conclusion: The Tao as a Guide to a Harmonious Life

"Be still, like a mountain, and flow, like a great river."
— Lao Tzu

Taoism offers profound wisdom for navigating life's complexities with grace, balance, and wisdom. Whether through the concept of Wu Wei, the balance of Yin and Yang, or the principle of non-resistance, Taoism teaches that the most effective way to live is to align ourselves with the natural flow of the universe. By letting go of the need for control, embracing balance, and yielding in the face of adversity, we find a path to peace, fulfilments, and lasting harmony.

In today's fast-paced and often chaotic world, the teachings of Taoism offer a refreshing reminder that life is not meant to be a constant struggle. Instead, it is an invitation to live in harmony with the world around us, to act with wisdom and humility, and to trust that when we move with the flow of life, rather than against it, everything falls into place naturally.

10

Buddhist Teachings – The Middle Path and Non-Attachment

Key Teaching: The Noble Eightfold Path – Right Understanding, Right Effort, and Right Action

"Do not dwell in the past, do not dream of the future, concentrate the mind on the present moment."
— *Buddha*

Central to Buddhism is the Noble Eightfold Path, a practical guide that outlines the way to end suffering and achieve enlightenment. The Eightfold Path encourages a life of balance and wisdom, known as the Middle Path, avoiding both extreme indulgence and severe asceticism. It is a comprehensive guide that touches on every aspect of life—thought, behaviour, and mindfulness. The path consists of eight interconnected elements: Right Understanding, Right Intent, Right Speech, Right Action, Right Livelihood, Right Effort, Right Mindfulness, and Right Concentration.

The three aspects most relevant to addressing conflict and choosing battles wisely are Right Understanding, Right Effort, and Right Action. These elements guide Buddhists in discerning which struggles are worth engaging in, and how to engage them without attachment or negative emotions.

- **Right Understanding** (Samma Ditthi) refers to seeing things as they truly are, recognising the Four Noble Truths—that suffering exists, that it arises from attachment, that it can cease, and that the path to its cessation is the Eightfold Path. This understanding allows individuals to see that life is inherently full of suffering (Dukkha), but that by following the Middle Path, we can reduce suffering for ourselves and others. Right Understanding helps us discern which struggles align with wisdom and which ones are driven by ego or ignorance.

- **Right Effort** (Samma Vayama) emphasizes the need for balanced effort in life's pursuits. It encourages putting energy toward cultivating good qualities—kindness, mindfulness, and compassion—while abandoning harmful ones such as anger, hatred, or greed. Right Effort also means focusing on battles that are grounded in ethical intentions, knowing when to let go of struggles that lead to suffering rather than inner peace.

- **Right Action** (Samma Kammanta) involves acting in ways that are moral, peaceful, and beneficial. It discourages violence, harm, or deceit, guiding individuals to choose actions that contribute to the welfare of others and to their own inner serenity. This part of the Eightfold Path teaches that not every conflict requires engagement; sometimes, non-action is the wisest and most compassionate choice.

For instance, in my own life, I've found that many of the daily struggles I engage in—arguments, professional rivalries, and even personal conflicts—are often driven by ego rather than true necessity. By reflecting on the principles of the Eightfold Path, I have learned to pause, assess the root cause of my struggles, and ask myself whether this conflict aligns with Right Understanding or Right Action. Often, I realise that letting go of the need to be right or to control outcomes leads to a greater sense of peace and clarity.

In a world that often glorifies constant striving and conflict, the teachings of the Noble Eightfold Path encourage us to approach life with wisdom, mindfulness, and ethical consideration. This balance leads to a more peaceful existence and helps us choose battles that are truly worth fighting.

Buddha's Rejection of Violence: Not Every Struggle Requires Conflict

"Holding onto anger is like drinking poison and expecting the other person to die."
— *Buddha*

One of the most profound teachings of Buddhism is the rejection of violence as a means to resolve conflict. The Buddha taught that violence only begets more suffering and that peace can be found in non-attachment and compassion. This is embodied in one of the core Buddhist precepts, Ahimsa, or non-violence. The Buddha believed that even though life is filled with struggles, not every struggle requires confrontation or aggression. Often, the wisest course is to practice patience, compassion, and non-attachment.

In Dhammapada 5, the Buddha says, "Hatred does not cease by hatred, but only by love; this is the eternal rule." This powerful teaching underlines the idea that engaging in conflict out of anger or hatred only perpetuates the cycle of suffering. Instead, Buddha urges us to meet conflict with understanding and love, breaking the cycle of violence and creating the conditions for peace.

One of the most notable examples of this principle in action is Buddha's own response to personal attacks and criticism. Rather than retaliating against those who insulted or wronged him, the Buddha maintained his inner calm and compassion. His response demonstrates that strength lies not in the ability to overpower others but in the ability to remain unmoved by anger and to choose compassion in the face of adversity.

This teaching is deeply relevant in today's world, where conflicts—whether political, social, or personal—often escalate into violence or hatred. Buddha's rejection of violence as a means to resolve conflict offers a path of peace, inviting us to step away from struggles that perpetuate suffering and instead cultivate understanding and compassion.

In my personal experience, I've found that many conflicts are rooted in miscommunication or misunderstanding. There have been times when I was tempted to respond with anger or frustration, but by reflecting on the Buddha's teachings, I learned to take a step back and approach the situation with patience and compassion. This not only diffused the conflict but also strengthened my relationships. The practice of non-violence and non-attachment has taught me that true power lies in self-control and inner peace.

Understanding Suffering as Part of Existence: Choosing Battles that Align with Inner Peace and Wisdom

> *"Pain is inevitable, but suffering is optional."*
> *— Haruki Murakami*

At the heart of Buddhism is the recognition that suffering (Dukkha) is an inherent part of existence. The Buddha's Four Noble Truths teach that life is marked by suffering, that suffering arises from attachment and craving, and that it can be overcome by following the Noble Eightfold Path. This understanding of suffering as inevitable helps individuals make wiser choices about which struggles to engage in and which to let go.

The Buddha emphasised that much of our suffering comes from attachment—to people, outcomes, possessions, or even ideas. When we become overly attached to things that are impermanent, we set ourselves up for disappointment and pain. Understanding this, the Buddha taught the practice of non-attachment as a way to free ourselves from unnecessary suffering. Non-attachment does not mean apathy or indifference; rather, it means releasing our obsessive grip on things that are beyond our control and focusing on what leads to peace and wisdom.

Dhammapada 277 captures this idea beautifully: "All conditioned things are impermanent—when one sees this with wisdom, one turns away from suffering." By recognising the impermanence of all things, we can better choose our battles, knowing that many struggles arise from our desire to control or hold onto things that are fleeting.

For example, in modern life, we often find ourselves caught in struggles over material wealth, status, or recognition. These desires can lead to endless frustration, competition, and unhappiness. The Buddha's teachings encourage us to step back and ask ourselves: Are these battles worth fighting? Do they lead to lasting peace and fulfilment? By choosing battles that align with inner peace and wisdom—rather than ego or attachment—we can live a more harmonious life.

I've seen this play out in my own life, particularly when it comes to career aspirations. Early in my career, I was driven by the desire for recognition and success, often feeling stressed and anxious about achieving my goals. But as I began to practice non-attachment, I learned to focus on the process rather than the outcome, letting go of the need for constant validation. This shift not only brought more peace into my life but also allowed me to engage in work that felt more aligned with my values and inner peace.

In today's world, where people are constantly encouraged to strive for more—more success, more possessions, more recognition—Buddhist teachings offer a counterbalance. By recognising the nature of suffering and practicing non-attachment, we can learn to choose battles that align with our deeper values, bringing more peace and wisdom into our lives.

Conclusion: The Middle Path as a Guide to Balanced Living

"Peace comes from within. Do not seek it without."
— Buddha

Buddhism teaches us that life is filled with suffering and challenges, but not every struggle is worth engaging in. By following the Middle Path—the balanced way of life that avoids extremes of indulgence and denial—and practicing non-attachment, we can choose battles that align with wisdom and inner peace. The Noble Eightfold Path provides us with the tools to live mindfully, to engage in struggles that serve a higher purpose, and to let go of those that only perpetuate suffering.

Buddha's rejection of violence and his emphasis on non-attachment remind us that true strength lies in our ability to meet life's challenges with patience, compassion, and wisdom. As we navigate the complexities of modern life, we can draw on these teachings to help us discern which battles to fight and how to fight them—always with the goal of reducing suffering and fostering peace, both within ourselves and in the world around us.

By choosing battles that align with Dharma—whether that means standing up for justice, showing compassion in difficult situations, or letting go of conflicts that arise from ego—we can live in a way that promotes harmony, wisdom, and lasting peace.

11

Myths and Legends – Symbolic Battles and Their Moral Lessons

The Power of Myths: Timeless Truths in Symbolic Battles

"Heroes are made by the paths they choose, not the powers they are graced with."
— *Brodi Ashton*

Throughout human history, myths and legends have served as powerful vehicles for conveying moral lessons, offering insight into the complexities of life, the nature of struggle, and the meaning of victory. These symbolic battles, found in the mythologies of different cultures, reflect timeless truths about the human condition and provide guidance on how to approach challenges with wisdom, perseverance, and a sense of purpose.

Myths are more than just stories; they are the collective wisdom of humanity, encapsulating our deepest fears, hopes, and values. They teach us that the struggles we face, whether internal or external, are part of a larger narrative of growth and transformation. In exploring these ancient tales, we find that the heroes' journeys are not so different from our own, and the lessons they learn can guide us in our own lives.

Greek Mythology: The Myth of Hercules and His Twelve Labours – Fighting for Redemption, Not Personal Glory

> *"Where there is no struggle, there is no strength."*
> — *Oprah Winfrey*

One of the most famous figures in Greek mythology is Hercules (Heracles), the demigod son of Zeus, known for his incredible strength and endurance. Yet, Hercules' greatest feats are not driven by a desire for personal glory but by his need for redemption. After being driven mad by the goddess Hera and killing his own wife and children, Hercules seeks atonement. As punishment for his actions, he is given twelve seemingly impossible tasks known as the Twelve Labours of Hercules, which he must complete to purify himself and regain his honour.

These labours, including slaying the Nemean Lion, capturing the Golden Hind of Artemis, and retrieving the apples of the Hesperides, symbolise the deep struggles of the human soul—the battle against inner demons, the pursuit of redemption, and the quest for self-improvement. Hercules' journey is not about seeking fame or power; it's about taking responsibility for his mistakes and working to right the wrongs of his past.

One of the key moral lessons from the myth of Hercules is that true strength lies in perseverance and moral fortitude. Hercules could have succumbed to despair after committing such a grievous sin, but instead, he chooses to take on the burden of his guilt and seek redemption through his actions. His twelve labours remind us that life's challenges are often opportunities for growth and transformation, and that the battle for redemption is one of the most honourable struggles we can undertake.

In today's context, we can see parallels in our own lives where mistakes or failures can feel overwhelming, tempting us to give up. However, like Hercules, we can choose to face our challenges head-on, working to correct our wrongs and seeking redemption through perseverance and right action. His story inspires us to view our struggles not as setbacks, but as opportunities for personal and moral development.

Norse Mythology: The Inevitability of Ragnarok – Fighting for the Greater Good, Even in the Face of Certain Defeat

> *"Sometimes even to live is an act of courage."*
> *— Seneca*

In Norse mythology, one of the most poignant and powerful themes is the inevitability of Ragnarok, the prophesied end of the world. According to legend,

Ragnarok will be a great battle in which the gods, led by Odin and Thor, will fight against the forces of chaos, led by the fire giant Surtur and the trickster god Loki. Despite knowing that the outcome of Ragnarok is predetermined and that they are fated to die, the gods still choose to fight valiantly, defending the cosmos and humanity until the bitter end.

The inevitability of defeat in Ragnarok is symbolic of the larger human experience, where we are all faced with the certainty of mortality and the limitations of our power. Yet, the gods' decision to fight regardless of their fate illustrates a profound moral lesson: that even in the face of inevitable defeat, it is still worth fighting for what is right and just. The battle is not about winning but about defending the greater good, preserving honour, and standing against chaos and destruction.

This concept of fighting for the greater good, even when victory seems impossible, is a powerful lesson in resilience and moral courage. It teaches that the value of a struggle does not lie solely in the outcome but in the integrity and bravery with which it is fought. The gods of Norse mythology know they will lose, yet they fight because it is their duty to uphold order and justice, even in the face of chaos.

In today's world, this lesson is especially relevant. Whether it's standing up for justice, fighting against systemic inequality, or advocating for environmental protection, there are battles that seem overwhelming and unwinnable. Yet, the story of Ragnarok reminds us that we must fight for what is right, not because we are guaranteed success, but because it is our duty to do so. The struggle for justice, truth, and the well-being of others is worth engaging in, even if the odds seem insurmountable.

This concept is echoed in movements for social justice, where activists continue to fight for change even when faced with long odds. The fight for civil rights, gender equality, and climate justice often feels like a never-ending battle, but like the Norse gods, individuals and communities persist, knowing that their efforts are meaningful, even if the ultimate victory is beyond their lifetime.

Native American Spirituality: Stories of Struggle for Survival, Wisdom, and Harmony with Nature

> *"We do not inherit the earth from our ancestors; we borrow it from our children."*
> — *Native American Proverb*

Native American spirituality is deeply rooted in stories and legends that emphasise the interconnectedness of all life and the importance of living in harmony with nature. Many of the stories from various Indigenous cultures involve struggles for survival, not just in the physical sense, but also in the spiritual sense—struggles to maintain balance, wisdom, and respect for the natural world.

One such story is the Lakota legend of White Buffalo Calf Woman, a sacred figure who brings the Lakota people the gift of the Sacred Pipe and teaches them how to live in harmony with the earth. In this story, White Buffalo Calf Woman appears during a time of great famine and suffering among the Lakota people. She provides them with the Sacred Pipe, which symbolises the connection between the people, the earth, and the Creator. The teachings she imparts emphasise respect for the earth, the importance of community, and the need to live in balance with all living things.

The struggles depicted in Native American myths often reflect the broader human challenge of maintaining harmony and balance, both within ourselves and with the environment around us. The battle for survival is not merely about physical endurance but about maintaining wisdom, respect, and humility in the face of hardship. Many Native American stories highlight the importance of understanding one's place within the natural world and the spiritual consequences of living out of balance.

This emphasis on harmony and balance is a crucial moral lesson in today's world, where environmental degradation, climate change, and the loss of biodiversity are pressing global issues. Native American spirituality teaches us that our struggles are not just about survival in a material sense but about maintaining a deep connection with the earth and all living beings. The battle to protect the environment is not simply about preserving resources for future generations—it's about living in harmony with the natural world and respecting the spiritual connections that bind all life.

In my own life, I've drawn inspiration from Native American teachings about the importance of mindfulness and respect for nature. I've come to understand that many of the struggles we face—whether personal or collective—are opportunities to restore balance and harmony. When faced with conflicts or challenges, reflecting on the wisdom of Native American stories helps me approach these situations with a sense of reverence for the interconnectedness of life and the need to act with integrity and respect for all living things.

Conclusion: The Moral Lessons of Symbolic Battles

> *"It is not our abilities that show what we truly are... it is our choices."*
> *— J.K. Rowling*

The symbolic battles in myths and legends from different cultures serve as powerful reminders that our struggles are often about more than personal gain or victory. They teach us that the real value of a battle lies in the moral and spiritual lessons it imparts—whether it's the quest for redemption, the fight for justice in the face of overwhelming odds, or the effort to live in harmony with the natural world.

- From Hercules' twelve labours, we learn that the greatest battles are often the ones we fight within ourselves, seeking redemption and moral clarity.

- From the Norse gods' fight in Ragnarok, we are reminded that even when defeat is inevitable, the fight for justice, honour, and the greater good is always worth engaging in.
- From Native American stories of harmony with nature, we understand that the battle for survival is deeply intertwined with the struggle to live wisely and in balance with the natural world.

These myths and legends offer timeless lessons that resonate with the challenges we face today, encouraging us to approach our own struggles with wisdom, perseverance, and a commitment to the greater good. Whether we are fighting internal battles, standing up for justice, or working to protect the environment, these stories remind us that every struggle carries the potential for growth, transformation, and moral clarity.

12

When God Fights for Us – The Role of Divine Assistance

The Concept of Divine Intervention Across Religions

"Be still, and know that I am God."
— Psalm 46:10

Across various religious traditions, the idea of divine intervention is central to stories of victory, protection, and justice. In moments of great struggle, when human strength alone is not enough, the intervention of the divine serves as a reminder that we are not alone in our righteous battles. Throughout sacred texts—from the Bible to the Quran and the Bhagavad Gita—there are numerous accounts of God or divine forces stepping in to aid those who fight for justice and righteousness.

The belief in divine assistance strengthens the idea that when we align ourselves with righteousness and moral duty, we invite the power of the divine to work on our behalf. These stories across religious traditions teach us that God fights for the just and the righteous, offering protection and guidance when our own efforts fall short.

Divine intervention refers to instances where a deity or supernatural force intercedes in human affairs, particularly in moments of crisis or moral conflict. In many religious traditions, divine intervention is seen as a response to the faithfulness of believers who are fighting for justice, morality, or the fulfilment of a divine plan.

In various holy scriptures, we see divine intervention taking different forms—whether it's God parting the Red Sea for the Israelites, angels descending to aid Muslim warriors, or Krishna guiding Arjuna on the battlefield. The underlying message is clear: those who align themselves with the will of God or the cosmic order are never truly fighting alone.

This belief in divine assistance inspires hope and perseverance in the face of adversity, especially when the odds seem insurmountable. It reassures us that when we commit ourselves to just causes and righteous struggles, we can count on a higher power to support us.

The Bible: Moses Parting the Red Sea with God's Power

"The Lord will fight for you; you need only to be still."
— *(Exodus 14:14)*

One of the most iconic examples of divine intervention in the Bible is the story of Moses parting the Red Sea, found in Exodus 14. The Israelites, after being freed from slavery in Egypt, find themselves trapped between the approaching Egyptian army and the Red Sea. In this moment of desperation, Moses cries out to God for help. God responds by instructing Moses to raise his staff over the waters, and by God's power, the sea parts, allowing the Israelites to cross safely. When the Egyptians pursue them, the waters close in, destroying the army and securing the Israelites' escape.

This miraculous event is not just a display of divine power but also a testament to God's willingness to intervene on behalf of His people when they are in peril. The parting of the Red Sea symbolises how God makes a way where there seems to be no way, fighting on behalf of those who are oppressed and leading them to freedom.

In this story, Moses is an instrument of God's will, and his faith in God's power is what allows the miracle to occur. Exodus 14:14 captures the essence of divine assistance: "The Lord will fight for you; you need only to be still." This powerful message reassures believers that when they are aligned with God's will, they need not rely on their own strength alone—God will intervene and fight for them.

This story continues to inspire people today, reminding us that in times of great difficulty, when we face obstacles that seem impossible to overcome, God is capable of delivering us through His power. Whether in personal struggles, moments of injustice, or times of great uncertainty, the story of the Red Sea parting reminds us that God fights for those who trust in Him and follow His guidance.

Quran: The Battle of Badr, Where Divine Angels Assisted Believers

"If Allah helps you, none can overcome you; and if He forsakes you, who is there after Him that can help you? In Allah, then, let believers put their trust."
— *(Surah Al-Imran 3:160)*

In Islamic tradition, the Battle of Badr stands as one of the most significant instances of divine intervention. This battle, which took place in 624 CE, was fought between the early Muslim community, led by the Prophet Muhammad, and the Quraysh, a much larger and better-equipped army. Despite being heavily outnumbered, the Muslim forces achieved a decisive victory, and it is believed that this was due to the intervention of divine angels sent by Allah to assist the believers.

Surah Al-Anfal 8:9 recounts this moment of divine assistance: "[Remember] when you asked help of your

Lord, and He answered you, 'Indeed, I will reinforce you with a thousand from the angels, following one another.'" The presence of these angels in the battle provided strength and encouragement to the Muslim warriors, reinforcing their faith and giving them the courage to fight against overwhelming odds.

The Battle of Badr is a powerful example of how divine intervention plays a role in the lives of those who fight for justice and righteousness. It teaches that when believers put their faith in God and commit themselves to just causes, they are not left to face challenges alone. Even in the most difficult circumstances, God's help is near, and His divine forces will support those who remain steadfast in their faith.

The story of the Battle of Badr is a reminder that God's assistance can come in many forms—whether through physical intervention, like the angels at Badr, or through spiritual strength and resilience that enables believers to persevere. This belief in divine support encourages Muslims to place their trust in Allah's will and continue fighting for what is right, even when victory seems impossible.

In my own life, I've often drawn inspiration from the story of the Battle of Badr when facing challenges that seemed overwhelming. Whether it's dealing with personal struggles or standing up for justice in difficult situations, the belief that God is with me, providing strength and guidance, has given me the courage to move forward with faith, knowing that I am not alone.

Bhagavad Gita: Krishna's Divine Intervention in Arjuna's Battle

"When your mind has overcome the confusion of duality,
you will attain the state of perfect peace
and unity in God."
— *Bhagavad Gita 2:53*

In Hindu tradition, the Bhagavad Gita stands as a sacred text that explores divine intervention, moral dilemmas, and the importance of righteous action. The central figure in the Gita, Arjuna, is a warrior prince who finds himself on the battlefield of Kurukshetra, torn by doubt and confusion about the morality of fighting a war against his own family members, teachers, and friends. In his moment of crisis, Lord Krishna, who serves as Arjuna's charioteer, reveals his divine form and delivers the teachings that make up the Bhagavad Gita.

Krishna's guidance to Arjuna is a profound example of divine intervention in times of moral conflict. Krishna explains to Arjuna that his duty (Dharma) as a warrior is to fight for justice and uphold righteousness, even when it comes at a great personal cost. He assures Arjuna that this battle is part of the larger cosmic order, and by fulfilling his duty without attachment to the outcome, he will align himself with the divine will.

In Bhagavad Gita 11:32, Krishna reveals his cosmic form and says, "I am time, the great destroyer of the world, and I have come here to engage all people." This revelation reassures Arjuna that the battle is not merely a human conflict but part of the divine plan. Krishna's intervention is not just about providing Arjuna with courage; it is about giving him the spiritual understanding to see his role in the larger scheme of things.

Krishna's divine intervention in the Bhagavad Gita teaches us that when we are aligned with Dharma—righteous duty—we can trust that the divine is guiding us, even when the path ahead seems fraught with moral complexity and personal loss. The Gita reminds us that the struggle for justice and righteousness is not a burden we carry alone; when we commit ourselves to the greater good, divine forces work alongside us.

In today's world, where we are often faced with difficult moral decisions, the Bhagavad Gita offers timeless wisdom. It teaches us to act with integrity, courage, and devotion to a higher purpose, trusting that when we fight for what is right, we are supported by the divine. Krishna's counsel to Arjuna reminds us that righteous struggles are never fought in vain and that divine assistance is always present for those who walk the path of Dharma.

How Righteous Struggles Align with Divine Will

"God does not look at your possessions, but at your heart and deeds."
— *Islamic Proverb*

Across these religious traditions, one common theme emerges: when we engage in righteous struggles—those that seek justice, uphold morality, and protect the vulnerable—we align ourselves with divine will. Whether it's Moses leading the Israelites to freedom, the Prophet Muhammad's believers standing firm at Badr, or Arjuna facing the moral complexity of war, these stories show that God fights for those who are committed to righteousness.

The concept of divine assistance is not just about miraculous interventions, but about the inner strength, wisdom, and courage that come from aligning with a higher purpose. When we pursue justice, truth, and compassion, we can trust that God is working through us and alongside us. This belief encourages people of faith to persevere in the face of adversity, knowing that their struggle is part of a larger, divine plan.

In my own life, I've found that when I act in accordance with my deepest values—whether standing up for justice, helping those in need, or speaking the truth—I feel a sense of divine support and guidance. Even in the most difficult moments, I've experienced a strength that I know does not come from me alone but from something greater.

Conclusion: God's Fight for the Just and Righteous

> *"The Lord is my light and my salvation*
> *—whom shall I fear?"*
> *— Psalm 27:1*

The stories of divine intervention across different religious traditions teach us that God fights for those who are aligned with justice and righteousness. Whether through parting seas, sending angels, or offering divine wisdom, God's assistance comes to those who stand up for what is right, even in the face of overwhelming odds. These stories inspire us to trust in divine support, knowing that when we engage in righteous struggles, we are never truly fighting alone.

As we navigate the challenges of life—whether personal, societal, or moral—we can draw strength from these teachings. They remind us that when we commit ourselves to righteous causes, we invite the power of the divine to work through us, guiding us, protecting us, and ultimately ensuring that justice will prevail.

13

Lessons on Discernment – Not Every Fight Is Your Fight

Choosing Battles Wisely Based on the Teachings of Religious Texts

"For everything there is a season, and a time for every matter under heaven."
— *(Ecclesiastes 3:1)*

In life, we are often faced with conflicts and challenges, and it can be difficult to determine when to engage in a struggle and when to step back. Religious teachings across various traditions emphasise the importance of discernment—the ability to choose our battles wisely, to know when a fight aligns with our moral and spiritual values, and to recognise when it's best to trust that a higher power will take over. This chapter explores how sacred texts guide us in making these decisions and offers insight into the role of hope, faith, and inner conviction in navigating life's challenges.

One of the key lessons found in many religious texts is the idea that not every fight is yours. While there are times when we are called to act in the face of injustice or to stand up for righteousness, there are also moments when the wisest course of action is to remain patient, allow divine justice to unfold, or walk away from conflicts that do not serve a greater purpose.

In the Bible, the story of David and Saul illustrates this principle beautifully. After David is anointed as the future king of Israel, King Saul grows jealous and repeatedly tries to kill him. On two occasions, David has the opportunity to kill Saul and claim the throne for himself, but he refrains, recognising that it is not his fight to take into his own hands. 1 Samuel 24:12 recounts David's words to Saul: "May the Lord judge between you and me, and may the Lord avenge the wrongs you have done to me, but my hand will not touch you." David discerns that vengeance belongs to God, not to him, and that waiting for God's timing is the righteous path.

This story teaches us that discernment involves humility and patience, trusting that God's justice will prevail in the right time. David understood that engaging in the wrong fight, even if it seemed justifiable, would have violated his moral integrity. By waiting for God to act, he allowed the divine will to unfold in a way that aligned with his righteousness.

Similarly, in Buddhist teachings, discernment is central to the Noble Eightfold Path, particularly in the practice of Right Action and Right Effort. The Buddha teaches that not every conflict or desire is worth pursuing, and that much of our suffering arises from engaging in struggles driven by attachment, anger, or ego. By practicing mindfulness and wisdom, we can choose which actions will lead to peace and enlightenment, rather than engaging in battles that perpetuate suffering.

The concept of Wu Wei in Taoism—acting by not acting—also emphasises that sometimes the best way to engage in life's challenges is to not force things. Taoist philosophy teaches that by aligning ourselves with the natural flow of life, we can let go of unnecessary struggles and trust that things will work out as they are meant to. Tao Te Ching 48 says, "In the pursuit of knowledge, every day something is added. In the practice of the Tao, every day something is dropped. Less and less do you need to force things, until finally, you arrive at non-action."

The principle of choosing battles wisely is about recognising that not every fight is worth our energy or time, and that some struggles are better left to unfold without our intervention. This wisdom encourages us to engage only in battles that align with our moral and spiritual convictions, and to let go of those that are driven by ego, pride, or fear.

Trusting that God, or the Divine, Will Fight for Justice When You Act with Righteousness

"Do not take revenge, my dear friends, but leave room for God's wrath, for it is written: 'It is mine to avenge; I will repay,' says the Lord."
— *Romans 12:19*

Another important lesson across religious traditions is the belief that when we act with righteousness, God or the Divine will fight for justice on our behalf. The role of divine intervention in human struggles is a central theme in many religious stories, teaching that when we align ourselves with justice, we are never truly fighting alone.

In Christianity, the belief that God fights for those who act justly is reflected in Romans 12:19, which says, "Do not take revenge, my dear friends, but leave room for God's wrath, for it is written: 'It is mine to avenge; I will repay,' says the Lord." This passage encourages believers to trust that God will bring justice in His time, and that we do not need to fight every battle ourselves. Our role is to act with righteousness, knowing that divine justice will follow.

In Islam, the Quran emphasises that those who remain steadfast in faith and fight for justice will have God's support. At the Battle of Badr, where the Muslim army was vastly outnumbered, divine intervention is said to have played a crucial role in their victory. Surah Al-Anfal 8:10 states, "And Allah made it not but good tidings and so that your hearts would be assured thereby. And victory is not but from Allah. Indeed, Allah is Exalted in Might and Wise." This reminds Muslims that God's assistance comes to those who fight for righteousness, and that ultimate victory comes from God's will.

In the Bhagavad Gita, Krishna's counsel to Arjuna on the battlefield of Kurukshetra reinforces the idea that when one acts in accordance with Dharma (righteous duty), divine forces align to support the struggle. Arjuna, conflicted about fighting in a war against his own family, is reminded by Krishna that his role is to act with righteousness, without attachment to the outcome. Bhagavad Gita 3:19 says, "Therefore, without being attached to the fruits of activities, one should act as a matter of duty, for by working without attachment one attains the Supreme."

Across these traditions, the lesson is clear: God fights for those who fight for justice. When we act in accordance with our moral and spiritual duties, we can trust that divine assistance will follow, and we do not need to force or control the outcome. This belief encourages hope and perseverance, knowing that our actions, when aligned with righteousness, are supported by a higher power.

The Importance of Hope, Faith, and Inner Conviction in All Struggles

> *"Faith is the assurance of things hoped for, the conviction of things not seen."*
> *— Hebrews 11:1*

While discernment teaches us that not every fight is ours to engage in, religious texts also emphasise the importance of hope, faith, and inner conviction in all struggles we face. These virtues are what sustain us through difficult times, reminding us that even when we step back from a battle or face overwhelming odds, our faith in a higher power will guide us through.

In the Bible, Hebrews 11:1 defines faith as "the assurance of things hoped for, the conviction of things not seen." This passage underscores the idea that faith is not about knowing the outcome of every struggle, but about trusting in God's presence and guidance, even when the path ahead is unclear. Faith gives us the strength to endure, knowing that God is with us in every step, whether we are called to fight or to wait.

Similarly, in Buddhism, the practice of Right Effort involves maintaining hope and determination in the pursuit of spiritual growth, even when challenges arise. The Buddha teaches that struggles are inevitable, but that with the right mindset—one of mindfulness, compassion, and non-attachment—we can move through those struggles with a sense of inner peace and conviction.

In Hinduism, the Bhagavad Gita emphasises the importance of Shraddha (faith) in fulfilling one's duties. Bhagavad Gita 17:3 says, "A man's faith conforms to the nature of his mind; whatever his faith is, that verily he is." This teaches that our faith shapes our actions and our identity, and that holding onto hope and conviction in the face of challenges is what allows us to persevere in the pursuit of Dharma.

In my own life, I've found that when faced with difficult decisions—whether to engage in a conflict or step back—it's my inner conviction, rooted in faith, that guides me. There have been times when I've chosen to walk away from a fight, trusting that the divine will bring justice in its own time. And in moments when I've chosen to engage, it was my faith that sustained me, giving me the strength to carry on despite the challenges.

Conclusion: Choosing Battles with Wisdom, Trusting in Divine Justice

The teachings of discernment from religious texts remind us that not every fight is ours to fight. Through wisdom and faith, we learn to choose battles that align with our moral and spiritual values, while trusting that God or the Divine will fight for justice when we act with righteousness. Whether through stepping back and allowing divine will to unfold or engaging in a struggle with hope and conviction, we can navigate life's challenges with a deep sense of trust.

The importance of hope, faith, and inner conviction in all struggles cannot be overstated. These virtues sustain us through uncertainty, reminding us that we are never truly alone in our battles. When we align ourselves with righteousness and act from a place of faith, we can trust that divine assistance is always near, guiding us through every challenge we face.

14

Conclusion:

Understanding Your Role in the Struggle for Good

Aligning Personal Struggles with a Greater Purpose

"Many are the plans in a person's heart, but it is the Lord's purpose that prevails."
— (Proverbs 19:21)

As we conclude, it's essential to reflect on the deeper meaning of our personal struggles and how they fit into the broader pursuit of goodness, justice, and righteousness. Life presents us with numerous challenges, and discerning which battles are ours to fight—and which we must entrust to a higher power—requires wisdom, faith, and a sense of purpose. Understanding our role in the struggle for good means recognizing the significance of aligning our actions with a greater purpose, balancing our efforts with divine reliance, and ultimately finding peace in the knowledge that good will prevail.

One of the key insights from religious teachings across traditions is the importance of aligning personal struggles with a greater purpose. Whether we are fighting for justice, navigating personal hardship, or seeking to overcome inner conflicts, the meaning and value of our efforts are amplified when they serve a cause greater than ourselves. When we focus not on personal gain, but on the larger pursuit of righteousness, our struggles take on a deeper significance.

In the Bible, we see this principle clearly in the story of Joseph. Sold into slavery by his brothers and unjustly imprisoned, Joseph could have been consumed by bitterness and self-pity. Instead, he recognised that his personal suffering served a greater purpose. In Genesis 50:20, he says to his brothers, "You intended to harm me, but God intended it for good to accomplish what is now being done, the saving of many lives." Joseph's ability to see his struggles within the context of God's larger plan allowed him to find meaning in his hardship and to become an instrument of good.

In the Bhagavad Gita, Krishna's counsel to Arjuna on the battlefield underscores the importance of aligning one's personal struggles with the cosmic order (Dharma). Arjuna's inner conflict is resolved when he realises that his duty as a warrior is not about personal glory or attachment, but about fulfilling his role in the greater cosmic plan for justice and righteousness.

Bhagavad Gita 18:47 says, "It is better to live your own Dharma imperfectly than to fulfil the Dharma of another with perfection." This teaching reminds us that when we align our personal struggles with a higher purpose, we contribute to the greater good, even if the outcome is uncertain.

In my own life, I've found that when I view my struggles through the lens of a greater purpose—whether it's standing up for justice in my community or supporting those in need—my efforts feel more meaningful. Even when the road is difficult, the knowledge that I am working toward something larger than myself provides the motivation and resilience to keep going.

The Balance Between Personal Action and Divine Reliance

"Trust in the Lord with all your heart and lean not on your own understanding; in all your ways submit to Him, and He will make your paths straight."
— Proverbs 3:5-6

Another crucial lesson from spiritual teachings is the need to strike a balance between personal action and divine reliance. While we are called to act with righteousness and integrity, we must also recognise our limitations and trust that divine forces are working alongside us. This balance is reflected in the concept that not every fight is ours to fight, and that some struggles are better left to the hands of God or the universe.

In the Quran, this balance is exemplified in the story of the Battle of Badr. Though the Muslim army was small and outnumbered, they fought with courage and relied on Allah for victory. Surah Al-Anfal 8:17 reminds the believers, "And you did not kill them, but it was Allah who killed them. And you threw not when you threw, but it was Allah who threw." This verse teaches that while human effort is necessary, ultimate success and justice come from divine intervention.

In Christianity, this balance is echoed in the teachings of Proverbs 3:5-6, which says, "Trust in the Lord with all your heart and lean not on your own understanding; in all your ways submit to Him, and He will make your paths straight." While we must take action in accordance with God's will, we are also called to trust that God is guiding our steps and working in ways that we may not fully understand.

The balance between personal effort and divine reliance is essential in today's world, where we often feel the pressure to control every aspect of our lives. Whether in our careers, relationships, or social causes, it's easy to become overwhelmed by the weight of responsibility. Yet, by recognising that our efforts are part of a larger divine plan, we can release the need to control outcomes and instead trust that our righteous actions will be supported by higher forces.

I've experienced this balance in my own life when facing challenges that felt beyond my control. By doing what I could with integrity and diligence, while simultaneously surrendering the outcome to God, I found peace in the process. This balance allowed me to act with confidence, knowing that I was not fighting alone.

Finding Peace in Knowing That Not Every Fight Is Ours to Fight, but That Good Ultimately Prevails

"The Lord will fight for you; you need only to be still."
— Exodus 14:14

Perhaps the most liberating lesson in the struggle for good is the realization that not every fight is ours to fight. We are not called to solve every problem or win every battle. Some struggles are beyond our control, and part of wisdom is knowing when to step back and allow divine will to unfold. This understanding brings a profound sense of peace, as it frees us from the burden of feeling responsible for outcomes that are not ours to determine.

In the Book of Exodus, when the Israelites are trapped between the Red Sea and the Egyptian army, Moses tells them, "The Lord will fight for you; you need only to be still" (Exodus 14:14). This powerful reminder encourages believers to trust that God is at work, even in moments of crisis. While we are called to act with righteousness, we must also recognise that God's timing and plan are perfect, and sometimes the best course of action is to wait and trust in divine justice.

In Taoism, the concept of Wu Wei (non-action) reflects a similar truth. Sometimes, the greatest wisdom lies in knowing when not to act, when to step back and allow the natural flow of the universe to bring about the right outcome. By not forcing solutions, we align ourselves with the Tao, trusting that all things will come to pass in their own time.

This lesson has been a source of peace in my own life, particularly when facing conflicts or challenges that felt beyond my ability to resolve. Recognising that not every battle is mine to fight has allowed me to let go of the anxiety that comes from trying to control every situation. Instead, I've learned to focus on what I can influence, while trusting that the greater forces at work will ensure that good ultimately prevails.

Conclusion: Good Ultimately Prevails

> *"The light shines in the darkness, and
> the darkness has not overcome it."*
> — *John 1:5*

As we reflect on our role in the struggle for good, it's important to remember that goodness and justice ultimately prevail—whether through our actions or through divine intervention. The journey toward righteousness requires discernment, faith, and perseverance, but it also requires humility in recognising that we are part of a larger, divine plan.

By aligning our personal struggles with a greater purpose, balancing our efforts with reliance on the divine, and finding peace in the knowledge that not every fight is ours to fight, we can navigate life's challenges with clarity and confidence. Religious teachings remind us that the ultimate victory belongs to the forces of good, and that when we act with righteousness, we are playing our part in bringing about that victory.

In the end, our role is not to control the outcome of every struggle but to act with integrity, faith, and hope, trusting that we are supported by something far greater than ourselves. Whether we are called to engage in a battle or to step back in trust, we can find peace in knowing that, in the grand scheme of things, good will always prevail.

About the Book

"Every Fight is Not Your Fight" delves into the profound wisdom found in religious texts across various traditions, guiding readers in discerning which battles are worth fighting and when to step back. Drawing from the Bible, Quran, Bhagavad Gita, and other spiritual sources, the book explores the role of divine intervention, personal action, and faith in the pursuit of justice and righteousness. It encourages readers to align their struggles with a greater purpose, trust in a higher power, and find peace in knowing that not every fight is theirs to engage in.

Reader Reviews

1. "A profound and insightful guide on discerning life's battles. Naresh Norbert CM masterfully weaves together wisdom from various spiritual traditions, offering practical lessons for everyday struggles. A must-read for anyone seeking clarity and peace."

   — *Rev. Dr. Job K Thomas CM, Educator and Author (Former Principal, De Paul School, Berhampur)*

2. "This book brings comfort and perspective. It teaches that not every challenge requires confrontation, and sometimes stepping back is the bravest act. The book is a beautiful and thoughtful reflection on faith and action."

   — *Rev. Dr. George Ayaloor CM, Bible Scholar*

3. "An inspiring journey through scripture and spirituality! Naresh Norbert CM shows how to align our struggles with a higher purpose, offering practical wisdom for those seeking balance between action and faith."

—*Rev. Dr. Pratap Chandra Misal CM, Philosopher and Scholar (Rector, Aquinas College, Gopalpur-On-Sea)*

4. "A rare gem that blends spiritual guidance with everyday practicality. The author's insights are both refreshing and deeply relatable, helping readers navigate life's challenges with grace and wisdom."

— *Sr. Justine Senapati SJA, Former UN Representative, Advocate for Social Justice and Human Right Activist*

About the Author

Fr. Naresh Chandra Nayak CM, a Catholic priest and former principal of De Paul School, Kolkata, is a dedicated member of the Congregation of the Mission. Hailing from Gajapati, Odisha, he holds a Bachelor's and Master's degree in English Literature, Bachelor's degree in Education and is a research scholar in English literature. Passionate about spreading faith and wisdom, he is an avid traveller, reader, singer, musician, and motivational speaker. In addition to his priestly duties, Fr. Naresh Chandra Nayak CM is also a content creator and writer, blending his academic background with his spiritual mission to inspire others.

www.ingramcontent.com/pod-product-compliance
Lightning Source LLC
LaVergne TN
LVHW041848070526
838199LV00045BA/1493